"It is not a lack of love, but a lack of friendship that makes unhappy marriages."
— *Friedrich Nietzsche*

FIX YOUR MARRIAGE IN 7 STEPS

A Practical Guide on How to Repair Your Marriage and Live a Happy Life With Your Spouse Ever After

Alice Gardner

BONUS LIBER

© Copyright 2020 by Alice Gardner - All right reserved.

The content contained within this book may not be reproduced, duplicated or transmitted without direct written permission from the author or the publisher. Under no circumstances will any blame or legal responsibility be held against the publisher, or author, for any damages, reparation, or monetary loss due to the information contained within this book, either directly or indirectly.

Legal Notice:

This book is copyright protected. It is only for personal use. You cannot amend, distribute, sell, use, quote or paraphrase any part, or the content within this book, without the consent of the author or publisher.

Disclaimer Notice:

Please note the information contained within this document is for educational and entertainment purposes only. All effort has been executed to present accurate, up-to-date, reliable, and complete information. No warranties of any kind are declared or implied. Readers acknowledge that the author is not engaged in the rendering of legal, financial, medical or professional advice. The content within this book has been derived from various sources. Please consult a licensed professional before attempting any techniques outlined in this book. By reading this document, the reader agrees that under no circumstances is the author responsible for any losses, direct or indirect, that are incurred as a result of the use of the information contained within this document, including, but not limited to, errors, omissions, or inaccuracies.

Contents

Introduction	1
1. What are the signs of a marriage in trouble?	5

    The Symptoms of a Marriage In Trouble
    What a Healthy Marriage Looks Like

2. Why Your Marriage Is Unhappy	11

    You Had Unrealistic Expectations of Marriage
    You Were Too Fearful to Share Your Feelings
    You Expected Your Partner to "Fix" You
    You Got Too Comfortable
    You Stopped Valuing Physical Intimacy
    You Refused to Give Each Other Space
    You Invited Mom and Dad Into Your Marriage
    You Dodged Important Conversations About Money
    You Started Oversharing Negative Thoughts
    You Treated Parenting as a Competition
    You Planned a Wedding, Not a Marriage

3. Reasons People Stay in Unhappy Marriages	25

    The Theory of the Frog
    Fear of Being Alone
    Fear of Judgment
    Fear of Causing Pain

Fear of Retaliation
Habit or Inertia
Staying for the Family
Wanting to Maintain Your Lifestyle
Religious or Cultural Beliefs
Feeling Unworthy of Better

4. A 7-Step Rescue Plan for Your Marriage   37
   Step 1: Communication
   Step 2: Conflict Resolution
   Step 3: Building Trust
   Step 4: Restoring Emotional Intimacy
   Step 5: Rekindling Physical Passion
   Step 6: Coping With Parenting Difficulties
   Step 7: Following Healthy Habits

5. Communication   45
   How Does Communication Work?
   Find the Right Time to Talk
   Speak Face to Face
   Stay Away from Attacking Each Other
   Be Honest
   Monitor Your Body Language
   Use the 48-Hour Rule
   Communicating When You Are Angry

6. Conflict Resolution   57
   Set a Primary Goal Together
   Set Boundaries
   Find the Real Issue
   Agree to Disagree
   Compromise When You Can

    Consider Everything
    Make the Necessary Changes

7. Building Trust   67
    Why Is Trust So Important to a Marriage?
    The Unexpected Ways Showing that Trust Is Broken
    The Necessary Steps for Rebuilding Trust
    Create a Sense of Understanding Between You Two
    Release All of the Anger You Are Feeling
    Provide Evidence of Your Commitment
    Rebuild Trust Through Practical Steps

8. Restoring Emotional Intimacy   81
    Emotional Intimacy is the Foundation
    Turning Off the Electronics
    Creating a Sense of Emotional Availability
    Increasing the Time You Spend Together
    Striking a Balance Between the Individual and the Couple
    Creating a "Fun List"
    Talking Through the Important Things

9. Rekindling the Spark   93
    Why You Need Sex in Your Marriage
    Making Time for Sexual Intimacy
    Communication and Copulation
    Forgiveness Fans the Flame of Passion
    Power of Non-sexual Touching
    Separating Sex From Routines
    Emotional Intimacy and Sex

10. Coping With Parenting Differences   103
    Discuss Your Parenting Expectations
    Create Rules for Your Parenting Practices
    Determine Consequences Together
    Support Each Other in the Parenting Process
    Never Disagree in Front of Your Children
    Be Flexible With Your Parenting Style
    Always Give Second Chances

11. Following Healthy Habits   111
    Talk on a Daily Basis
    Schedule Time for Each Other
    Kiss Each Other Every Day
    Consult One Another
    Openly Express Your Gratitude
    Genuinely Listen to Your Partner
    Go on Regular Dates
    Spend Time Reminiscing

12. Keeping Your Marriage Off Life Support   121
    Commit Seriously to Your Marriage
    Respect and Honor Your Partner
    Schedule Time for Honest Communication
    Share Your Financial Expectations
    Make Space for Yourselves and Each Other
    Manage Your Wellness Together
    Work on Forgiving Each Other Quickly
    Avoid Trying to Control Each Other
    Keep Practicing Healthier Marital Skills

Conclusion   131

Introduction

Everyone knows that marriage is one of the most beautiful and most heartfelt commitments we make in our lives; at the same time, it can turn out to be one of the most challenging, overwhelming, and triggering relationships to navigate. I want to give you the relief that all couples that I've helped throughout my career have gone through difficult settling-in periods and painful growth at varying stages in their relationships. For some couples, these periods can become extremely tough and might lead to a lot of hurt feelings and friction in the relationship.

It goes without saying that you do love your partner, you cherish them, value them, appreciate them, and are grateful to have them in your life. But sometimes, like anybody else, they can be tough to be with. It may be because they tend to push all your buttons in the wrong ways or because you are not communicating that those buttons exist. In many cases, it is a combination of both. And when one partner is unhappy, you can be confident that probably both partners are unhappy.

When you reach this stage in your relationship, you have two options.

You can pack up and leave.

Or, you can calm down, sit and want to figure out where the root of your issues lies and begin to handle and resolve them.

Of course, there is no right or wrong answer. If you have reached a point in your relationship where you genuinely cannot imagine yourself with your partner anymore, and there is no hope for your future together, it might be time to call it quits. But since you are here reading *Fix Your marriage in 7 Steps*, I can infer that you are not there yet. You are willing to work it out together and improve your relationship.

Needless to say that you desire that loving, magical bond with your partner, and you want to continue spending the rest of your life with them. That's why you are here, ready for confrontation and willing to deal with your issues and figure out how you can return to that happy state. Despite your past, you and your spouse can forgive each other, improve your foundation, and move forward in harmony. That is what *Fix Your marriage in 7 Steps* will teach you.

In this book, I will discuss the practical steps you can take to help you upgrade the quality of your marriage. Reading this book will help you reach a point where you and your partner just know how to handle the issues, anytime your relationship is on the verge of going through difficulties. In addition, you will find yourselves enjoying a healthier and more stable connection that reflects your mutual love, understanding and happiness.

Before we get started, I want to say that I am heartily thankful to you for being here and having decided to work on your relationship with your partner. It takes a lot of courage and strength to move through adversity and hard times, let alone move through challenges with another person in such an intimate way. Obviously, being vulnerable with your partner and yourself, while facing these challenges is definitely tricky. Yet, this is one of the most powerful steps you can take toward enjoying a stronger and healthier connection with your partner. If all you have right now is hope for a better future, then you have plenty to make this work.

We are about to focus on filling in the steps you are going to take in order to turn that hope into tangible success. If you are ready to *Fix Your Marriage in 7 Steps,* turn the page!

CHAPTER 1

What are the signs of a marriage in trouble?

Marriages are often depicted as romantic, life-long relationships of love and joy shared between two best friends. When they are at their best, marriages are a safe, passionate, peaceful place to belong to for both partners involved. They have all of the elements you need to feel secure in your connection with your significant other, while also feeling empowered to be yourself and develop as an individual. Of course, marriage is a magical place to be, except when it shows signs of illness.

When a marriage starts showing those warning signs, it can begin to feel like you are carrying a heavy burden on your shoulders. You might start feeling the growing pressures of taking care of yourselves, each other, and the relationship you share. With so many moving aspects of that relationship, it may feel too overwhelming to take the necessary steps to get back to a healthy place. Couples in a lousy place often feel as though they fail as spouses, friends, parents, family members, and any other role they may play in their marriage with their partner. This can be incredibly painful and can make saving yourself and your relationship from that challenge seem impossible.

I recommend stepping back and notice the exact symptoms of illness before you start to navigate them, as this will help you come up with a game plan. This plan determines your course of action and enables you to apply the magic seven steps in a practical and enduring way. If you follow it correctly, you will heal your relationship from the inside out, creating a safe space for both you and your significant other.

The Symptoms of a Marriage In Trouble

My fellow therapists, including myself, believe that most couples don't notice that their marriage is going through difficulties until it is in serious trouble. They start seeing the symptoms of a problem just after the crisis already matured, rather than when the issue was still fresh and probably easier to resolve. Had that couple navigated the situation more effectively early on, it would not have turned into severe trouble. Their inability to face the issue promptly, however, leads to more severe issues.

If you are in the early stages of trouble in your marriage, the symptoms are subtle. You begin to feel disconnected from your partner, your interactions with each other change drastically, and small feelings of hurt and annoyance start to develop. It may be difficult to notice at first because the troubles are so small that you are sure you can shrug them off, but they tend to grow over time. Soon, you feel like you are always shrugging things off, and your partner doesn't seem to care that you are doing this. They may even feel the same way. You might start sitting on different ends of the couch, ignoring each other, looking at your phones or finding separate hobbies, failing to schedule quality time together, and letting your connection slowly drift apart. Even though you live under the same roof, you might feel like you are a million miles apart.

As the feelings of disconnect grow, the feelings of hurt and rejection develop as well. You find yourself feeling hurt that your partner seems to be rejecting you and that they are not as attentive and compassionate toward you as they used to be back in the day. You notice that you behave similarly toward them and their need for attention and compassion.

The continuation of these behaviors toward each other leads to many additional symptoms of trouble in your marriage. You start constantly bickering, withdrawing from each other in sarcastic and even mean ways, fighting unfairly, having the same arguments repeatedly, and escalating your arguments until they are out of control. You might start to feel as though you have different desires, goals, and expectations, to the point where you end up sensing some sort of inequality around who's opinions matter the most.

In extreme cases of troubled marriages, the relationship can become incredibly toxic. You stop trusting each other, respecting each other, and finally loving each other. You may start lying to each other, seeking positive attention from someone else or feeling like your partner does not care about you or want to be around you. At the lowest point of a problematic relationship, it might seem like you both hate each other, and the connection is the most dreaded part of your life. It might seem like the only hope for happiness is to leave each other, and in some cases, that may be true. But even in the direst situations, where something terrible like name-calling or infidelity has occurred, healing is absolutely possible, and you can go on to enjoy a happy, healthy marriage. It all starts with first analyzing whether you genuinely want this for yourself and believe you can have a happy marriage with this person again.

I want to tell you that you just need to know in your heart that you want to find a way to forgive your partner and enjoy a happy marriage together. If you can believe in this, your relationship can definitely heal and thrive once again.

What a Healthy Marriage Looks Like

Dear reader, remember that a healthy marriage looks totally different from how it is often depicted by media. In healthy marriages, spouses act like best friends and spend a great deal of quality time together, building their relationships. They enjoy being in each other's company, and it may even seem like they do everything together. However, there is far more to marriage, and life, than just the moments you spend with your partner. While enjoying each other's company and doing things together is a valuable way to build your relationship, many different steps can lead to a healthy, long-lasting connection with your partner.

In addition to spending quality time together, healthy marriages consist of two people willing to discuss their problems respectfully and navigate them in a way that works for both. Healthy relationships are never void of conflict or disagreements. Instead, the conflict must exist to some extent in order to prove that both partners value each other and their happiness and are ready to resolve the issues together. If you have a dispute in a healthy relationship, you may not like your partner's opinion or position on something, but you agree to navigate it respectfully. Look for ways you can both win, and always be kind to each other. Your number one goal is for both of you to be happy and receive all of the fulfillment you need from your shared relationship.

Another way through which marriages are made healthy, in my opinion, is the element of independence. Having a certain dependency on your partner in marriages is inevitable since you share so much. Still, your entire life and well-being should not be dependent on your partner. Likewise, their life and well-being should not be dependent on you. Each of you should have hobbies that you do separate from each other. These independent experiences allow you to remain healthy and confident by yourself. That will enable you to show up as a whole, happy person in your relationship with your partner. The combination of love, respect, compassion, and trust enables both partners to enjoy a happy, healthy relationship.

Chapter 2

Why Your Marriage Is Unhappy

I totally understand! Realizing that your marriage is in trouble is a hard pill to swallow. You might start wondering where you went wrong, what happened that led you down this path, or why you are no longer on the same page in many issues. It can be easy to jump into panic mode when you find out that your once-thriving relationship is now in a dangerous or toxic place and that it needs to be saved. You might wonder if you can even save your relationship in the first place. Remember, as long as you can visualize a future where you and your partner have forgiven each other, learned to treat each other better, and moved on, even if you don't know how you will get there, there is hope.

Uncovering why your marriage has become unhappy is how you start to repair it. This way, you are working directly on the troubles you encounter, rather than wasting your time trying to resolve problems that are not at the root of your issue. When your relationship is in danger, immediate changes are required so that both you and your partner can start to feel safe, loved, and cherished once again. As these elements come back, the rest of the relationship can start to heal, and you can enjoy your lives together afresh.

You Had Unrealistic Expectations of Marriage

Divorcing couples often reach that state because they failed to accept their spouse, themselves, or their relationship. Many couples meet, date for a while, fall in love, and then get married. It is often said that love and respect are the two most significant factors in a marriage, but acceptance is just as essential. Failing to accept your partner or the relationship you share will virtually always lead to bickering. You continue to hold your partner against expectations that they cannot reasonably meet. The longer your expectations go unmet, the less happy you are with the relationship, and the more strain grows between you.

I don't want to imply that having expectations of your partner and marriage is a bad thing. On the contrary, expectations help you understand what you want and need from your marriage and allow you to communicate those needs to your partner, which is definitely healthy. When you have unrealistic expectations of your partner or your relationship, you start to run into issues with your marriage.

If you are disappointed because you thought that marriage was only about butterflies, bouquets, and hot passionate sex for the rest of your life, you are actually frustrated due to your own unrealistic expectations. The reality is that marriage is a lot more than just hot, fiery emotions and feelings of falling in love. Marriage is love, family, stability, peace and comfort. There can be burning, passionate moments, but most of the time, it will be more relaxed and easy-going than that. Unfortunately, this pace can often lead to boredom and contempt, as well as feeling as though you have been rejected by your partner who, at one time, could not seem to get enough of you. This is all normal, though, and can be worked through. Once you have realistic expectations of your partner and your marriage, you can start looking forward to a better relationship that feels happier, safer, and more fulfilling.

You Were Too Fearful to Share Your Feelings

I totally get that! Sharing your feelings is scary, no matter who you are and who you want to share your emotions with. Even if you love and cherish your partner, talking about those profound, dark aspects of your emotional self can feel intimidating. It might feel impossible to admit that you are feeling hurt, rejected, jealous, or insecure. You might feel like your partner does not care or does not listen to you when, in reality, you were unable to share your real thoughts and emotions because you were only scared.

No matter how long you have been with your partner or how close you have been in your lifetime, fear can pop up and make things difficult. We all have aspects of our emotional selves that are overwhelming, difficult to understand, and even harder to share with others. Despite knowing that your partner would likely understand, it can be challenging to admit your feelings and talk them through with your spouse. You might fear being judged, not being accepted, or treated differently, which could lead to feeling rejected and unwanted. The more you sit in this fear, the more challenging it becomes to navigate it, and consequently, the less you may feel confident in your relationship. Needless to say, that over time, this can seriously destroy your marriage.

It takes time, work, and it may take some communication about your feelings of fear before you dig into the emotions you were scared of sharing in the first place, but even your most profound and scariest fears can be overcome. If your partner is open to receive you, and you honestly share with them, you can recover from these challenges and experience an even stronger relationship with your partner. Through this, your connection will become stronger as well as more durable than ever before.

You Expected Your Partner to "Fix" You

It's sad but true! Throughout my career, I have met so many people who get married, hoping and believing that their partner can "fix" them. Expecting your spouse to heal you is a surefire way to set your marriage up for failure. The trouble with this particular issue is you may not even realize that you have expected your partner to fix you until after you have examined how you have been behaving throughout your relationship.

Never get into a relationship hoping that your spouse will fulfill the needs that your parents didn't, as this creates an unfair and unrealistic burden for your partner to carry. No matter what your partner does, they will likely always get it wrong in your eyes because they will never be able to fill the void you are trying to fill. Eventually, your partner will become frustrated with you for continually having such high expectations that they cannot fulfill, and more importantly, it will erode your marriage in the long run.

If you have already been partaking in this toxic cycle, it is time for you to change your dynamic. Otherwise, your marriage will remain poisonous and eventually end in a devastating way, rather than with a quiet and respectful decision to part ways.

You Got Too Comfortable

Comfort, naturally, can be a good feeling to experience in a relationship. However, if you get too comfortable, you can destroy your relationship from the inside out. Comfort can destroy relationships by making partners complacent and allowing them to feel like they no longer have to try. One or both partners will often become lazy and stop trying to impress their spouse, and take each other for granted, a process that results in their spouse beginning to feel like they have never been treated as unique as they used to be. In marriages or any romantic relationship, unique treatment helps build intimacy and keeps the relationship vital. You must always be willing to show up and put effort into it in order to be able to keep your relationship stable and gratifying.

It may feel uncomfortable or unnatural at first, but you have to put that same energy into keeping your partner as you did in the beginning. Take care of yourself, groom yourself for your partner, continue trying to impress them, and put effort into catching their attention. Flirt like you have recently met each other and do all of the same things that made you fall in love with each other in the first place. When you put this effort into your relationship, your attraction grows over time, rather than peaking and simmering. As a result, your relationship stays pleasant, cheerful and intimate for the years to come.

You Stopped Valuing Physical Intimacy

Avoiding physical intimacy can sometimes lead to infidelity or divorce. When you do not have a good sex life with your partner, it is easier to give up on your marriage because it no longer feels like you share what keeps marriages going. That is the unique, personal connection that you two share, and it's exclusively yours. Often, the majority of things we share with our partner can also be shared with other people. We can love, have inside jokes, enjoy, and engage in unique, intimate relationships, but physical intimacy is something we have only with our partner.

It is beautiful to be great companions, friends, and even co-parents, but you must have something special that you share beyond that. In reality, if you lack physical intimacy, your spouse begins to look like your roommate rather than your spouse, and you begin to feel resentful about that, and the situation gets more complicated and

Although the sexual aspect of a relationship does not have to be everything, and obviously there shouldn't be obligations and pressures to have sex, you need to get to the root of the matter and start examining physical intimacy again. Learn how to hold hands, cuddle, and engage in varying degrees of physical intimacy. Then, when you are comfortable, incorporate sex back into your relationship. Eventually, it will feel as passionate and sexy as it ever did, and your relationship will begin to thrive again.

You Refused to Give Each Other Space

I believe that physical closeness is essential, but so is giving and receiving adequate space. Even though your relationship may be one of the essential things in your life, it is crucial to realize your freedom is equally important. You might not feel like it, but after too much time without independence, you will begin to feel suffocated and resent your partner for always being around or vice versa. Unfortunately, many people do not realize the essential need for personal space and do not recognize the importance of having this time to be independent and on their own.

If you are beginning to resent each other or are having a hard time, it can be helpful to consider taking time apart. Engaging in independent hobbies, doing things on your own, and even taking separate vacations or trips is an excellent way to create a sense of space between you and your partner. This space may seem scary at first, especially if you clung to your partner because of fear of losing them or abandonment issues, but remember that there is a reason that the proverb 'absence makes the heart grow fonder' was created in the first place, so follow it and give your hearts that precious opportunity. Once you are apart for a while, you can start to remember all of the beautiful reasons why you fell in love with your partner at the start. You may even flirt with them while you are away and find yourself looking forward to being with them again when you come back.

Absence also allows you to start to build a greater sense of confidence with your partner. Suppose your trust has eroded over the years. In that case, this is an excellent opportunity to rebuild your relationship with new, reasonable rules that can help restore confidence and deepen your connection as well.

You Invited Mom and Dad Into Your Marriage

I can understand that going through trouble in your relationship can be a challenge. You might feel like you need to vent to someone, and for many people, that person to vent to is mom or dad. While venting can help you feel more peaceful and calm you down, it is essential to realize that certain people should be off-limits for venting. Further, venting should always be done in a way that is respectful to your partner.

Let me get this straight! Your parents, or anyone in your family, will never be the right people to confide in about the issues you may be going through with your partner. Often, they will see even the smallest troubles as significant issues and will either make unfair judgments about your partner or try to manipulate your relationship to help you out. But I want to assure you that neither of these will ever help. All of it only leads to more strain on your relationship by having interference from family members who do not have complete knowledge of your partner or your marriage.

You must always respect your partner enough to speak to them directly about your troubles. If you can't do that, talk to a friend you trust and let them know you just need to vent or seek help from a good therapist. These individuals are far more likely to refrain from judging your partner or interfering in your relationship, which will lead to better outcomes from the troubles you are facing right now.

You Dodged Important Conversations About Money

Money is well-known for destroying marriages, and it happens frequently. Further, the issue of money can rapidly obliterate any marriage in several different ways, ranging from other goals to misaligned spending habits. Perhaps the saddest stories are of those where couples spent so much money on their weddings that they started their marriage with financial problems and ended up getting divorced. But let me tell you this, that even later into the marriage, money can become an issue.

Talking money with your partner is challenging but essential. It is a conversation you need to have before you even get married, and it is a conversation you need to keep having throughout the marriage. Money is an emotional topic, and it can make people feel defensive, fearful, embarrassed or even resentful toward others. If you and your partner disagree on how finances will be managed, including how they will be earned, saved, spent, and otherwise used, it can be a warning sign of future problems in this regard. You need to discuss this as soon as possible and reach an agreement so both you and your partner can prevent problems regarding money to pop up.

It is vital that you build a budget together that reflects your financial goals and feels achievable for both of you, and that you work toward that budget regularly. You should also consistently save some money if an emergency should come up and review your finances every now and then to ensure things are going well. The more you face your finances head-on as a couple, the fewer arguments you will have about money.

You Started Oversharing Negative Thoughts

Negative thoughts pop into our heads. Everyone experiences negative thoughts, and sometimes those thoughts can last hours, days, weeks, or even months, especially if undesirable circumstances seem to be feeding into those thoughts. It's actually normal to have negative thoughts, but oversharing them is something you should avoid. In a relationship, there are the forbidden four C's of negative thoughts, which should always be avoided, no matter how you might be feeling or what you might be thinking. These forbidden four C's include complaining, criticizing, unproductive conflict, and condemning (including accusing, blaming, insulting, labeling, and other forms of condemning.)

While I totally encourage you to speak your mind, it is also essential that you verbalize yourself in a way that is kind, compassionate, and respectful to your partner. Learn how to vocalize your thoughts and feelings in a way that expresses how truly upset you are about something without tearing your partner down. Be assertive, clear, and concise in your sharing, be kind, and look for productive results from your conversation. Anytime you speak to be mad or hurtful, you are doing a disservice to your partner, yourself, and your marriage.

Anytime you start to get angry, take responsibility for your anger, and give yourself time to understand why you have become so mad in the first place. Once you have sorted through your emotions, give yourself a chance to identify how you can manage to share these thoughts and feelings in a kind, respectful manner, and then do so. You will find that you resolve conflict far more effectively this way, and you both feel much better when you do this.

You Treated Parenting as a Competition

You might have repeatedly heard that becoming parents changes a marriage. But have you ever asked yourself why that is? Here is my answer: once you become parents, there are entirely new people introduced to your family unit, and they are people that you are responsible for. It is essential to realize that even if you have similar beliefs about raising children, you will always be on different pages about some things. You must learn how to communicate and compromise as parents, rather than viewing parenting as a competitive activity. Never try to compete with your partner in this regard, nor undermine their performance as a parent. If you have issues you do not agree upon, address them with each other *before* discussing them with your children.

Remember that both of you have an equal part in raising your children; as a result, both of you deserve to have an equal say in how they are raised. The useful piece of advice I can give you regarding this matter is that you need to respect each other in all circumstances and always look for ways to ensure that both you and your partner are satisfied with how parenting is being proceeded and performed. This way, you can operate as a working team and support each other in successful parenting, rather than tearing each other apart and harming your children, which is an extremely destructive side effect.

You Planned a Wedding, Not a Marriage

I have observed throughout my career that an alarming number of couples get together, fall in love, and discuss everything about their *wedding*. They never pause to think about what comes after or consult the topic of their actual *marriage*. After the wedding, what we have got is two people eager to be together and share one special day but not yet prepared to spend the rest of their lives together with wisdom, mindfulness and open eyes.

The good news I'm going to give away to you is that even if you are already married, you can pause and start to have these critical conversations with your partner. Discuss your preferences around having and raising children, your originating families, methods for handling conflict, religion, finances, privacy concerns, household chores, each other's love languages, and your future goals. You should also discuss your troubles or baggage and what your hopes are for the future.

Before getting married, I encourage you to have in-depth conversations about all of these fundamental issues, since it is a great way to build a fair and realistic vision of what your life looks like, and hopefully enables you to start planning a marriage together. Even if you are already married, consider discussing the essential matters with your spouse at the right time.

Chapter 3

Reasons People Stay in Unhappy Marriages

From the outside, when you see two people in an unhappy marriage, you might see their breakup to happen very soon, and it's something obvious to you. However, it does not always feel that obvious to people inside of the relationship. Further, breaking up is not always the answer to an unhappy marriage, as most marriages can be repaired if both parties are willing to invest the time and energy into making it work.

The trouble comes when both partners refuse to leave, but they also cannot seem to bring happiness back into their marriage. However hard they try, they may not be able to move past the resentment, hurt, disappointment, feelings of rejection, or other painful experiences they have had inside their marriage. This often means that they struggle to embody forgiveness, so they find themselves trapped in a situation where they are unsure whether they should stay or leave. As a result, they find themselves living permanently at this state of impasse, remaining disappointed yet unwilling or unable to do anything about it.

Knowing why you are in an unhappy marriage is as important as knowing why your marriage has become a burden in the first place. The more you understand why it got here, the easier it will be for you to figure out where to go next.

The Theory of the Frog

One of the best theories that explain why people stay in troublesome situations is defined with the story of the frog in water. The metaphor is as follows: if you put a frog in boiling water, it will immediately jump out. If you put a frog in cold water and slowly bring it to a boil, the frog will not try to jump out until it becomes too hot. At that point, the frog cannot jump out because the heat has caused too much damage to their system. They are effectively trapped and will die in the boiling water.

The theory is that humans experience something similar in the relationships they engage in. If they jump into a relationship that is troublesome from the start, they would immediately recognize that and leave that situation in search of a more comfortable one. If, however, they were to jump into a relationship that was wonderful and deteriorated over time, they may stay and may become unable to recognize and determine what they really need or want. They continue to the point that eventually, they will essentially become trapped in that deteriorated relationship.

Most marriages do not start badly. Instead, they start excellent and deteriorate over time as both partners slowly find their way into a bad situation. Often, one or both partners start holding back on their opinions or failing to communicate their needs. One or both partners might also fail to consider the feelings and conditions of the other, causing them to act in an unkind or uncompassionate manner. These issues may be small at first, but they build over time and, eventually, the anger becomes significant and impossible to hide. Before either person realizes it, they are experiencing significant issues in their relationship, and it seems as though they have struck out of nowhere. The reality is, the problems had been there for a long time, but they were gradual in their development until they reached the point where they could no longer be ignored.

Once you see the primary signs of unhappiness in your marriage, you might wonder why you are staying in your marriage. Research has shown that there are many reasons why people stay in unhappy marriages, ranging from fear of being alone to genuinely loving each other and genuinely wanting to fix things but not knowing how. Ten significant reasons are responsible for people staying in unhappy marriages, and they are as follows.

Fear of Being Alone

Fear of being alone is a significant reason why people stay in unhappy marriages. Many people are not alone for long in their lives, as they grow up with family, move out, and meet their partners shortly after. Though they may go a few years living independently, they are often not lonely for long. Those who are alone for more extended periods may be afraid to go back to that for fear of being alone for even longer. In either scenario, you may find yourself not wanting to leave your partner because you are afraid of being alone, and you are unsure how to cope with being by yourself.

If you fear being alone, it could result in staying in an unhappy marriage because you are afraid of walking away and being without your partner. It could also make you stay in an unhappy marriage as you feel like you *have* to be there to be comfortable, and that feeling of obligation can render working on your marriage even more challenging. In this case, even if you wanted to stay, you might begin to experience low self-esteem, and you start to question if you genuinely want to stay or if you are just afraid of being alone.

Fear of Judgment

Needless to say that our family and friends play a significant role in how we feel about ourselves. If you are in an unhappy marriage, you might be so afraid of other people's judgment that you refuse to do anything about it. You might fear that if you leave your spouse, your family will judge you for a number of reasons, from not making it work to not making up your mind. That fear of judgment can keep you trapped in an unhappy marriage and feeling as though you cannot even mention your unhappiness.

Fear of being judged by others not only can make you reluctant to leave your unhappy relationship, but also can make you unable to work on your relationship because of the shame you have developed around your unhappiness. Let me get this straight; the first step to healing and going forward is that you must try to accept your present unhappiness in your marriage. This acceptance ensures that you are ready to either leave or take the necessary action to improve your marriage and enjoy a healthier connection with your partner. Of course, I understand that it is never pleasant to live in a situation where you are ashamed of your unhappiness, as shame can be distressing, and that distress can prevent you from healing your unhappy circumstances.

Fear of Causing Pain

If you are afraid of causing pain to your partner, or anyone else who may be impacted by your marriage, you might stay in an unhappy marriage. Fear of causing pain stems from fear of conflict, and it often leads to people not speaking up about their feelings, needs, or concerns because they do not want to cause pain to someone else. This fear can lead to staying in a marriage that you do not want to be in, and it can also lead to refusing to take the necessary actions to improve your marriage so it can be more pleasant and enjoyable for both of you.

If you are afraid of causing pain, the necessary thing to do is telling it to your partner. Tell them that you are worried that your decisions or hesitations may cause them pain and hurt. You may genuinely feel like you want to leave, or you may find that you want to stay, but you are afraid of telling your partner that the relationship is not working for you. Either way, you absolutely need to talk about it and start working toward finding a solution so you can both be freed from the unhappy circumstances and find your way into a happier marriage.

Fear of Retaliation

Some people, especially those in toxic relationships, may be so scared to leave their partners because they fear retaliation. If you are afraid that your partner will try to do something to hurt you, like take your children away or harm you in some way, you have the right to be afraid to leave your marriage because who wants to be hurt?! Of course, nobody. If you find yourself in this situation, you need to ask yourself if your fear is real. You may realize that your anxiety could be carried over from previous relationships or a toxic experience you had in the past, or that your alarm is valid, and your partner is likely to retaliate and attempt to harm you or your family if you plan to leave them.

If you find yourself in this situation, the only solution is to leave the marriage. That will not be easy; however, you have to find a way to protect yourself from the possible retaliation they may attempt. Surround yourself with people you trust and love and those who can protect you and provide a safe place for you and your children, or contact a local battery shelter or non-profit organization designed to help people who are in dangerous marriages and relationships. This will help you plan your escape so you can go without being harmed by the possible retaliation. Never ever stay in a relationship where this behavior is present since you will never be able to turn it into a happy or safe marriage.

Habit or Inertia

Humans are creatures of habit since habit creates pleasure and momentum. It can be easy to resist change since you are used to being in this relationship. You might even find yourself denying that the relationship is as bad because you have become so used to it that it feels familiar. If you are on autopilot and stay in your marriage out of habit and comfort, you need to start repairing the situation by focusing on these perceived feelings of comfort. Take an honest look at your relationship and recognize where the toxicity and trouble have found a way in, and start looking for ways to adjust your habits so you can change your situation for the better.

Sometimes you need to leave your relationship since the only reason you are staying is the fear of changing your habits. On the other hand, you might reach this conclusion that your relationship will be significantly improved if you break free from the habits and start taking real action toward happiness in your relationship. In either case, you need to find a way to step out of your habits and create a higher level of joy in your life.

Staying for the Family

If you have a family together, or if you particularly enjoy your partners' family, you might find that you are tempted to stay in a relationship because you do not want to lose your circle. You might worry that your children would be badly affected and even devastated to have their parents divorced, or that your relationships with your spouse's parents would fall apart. These fears can keep people in relationships since they do not want to lose the family dynamic they have built over time.

Staying in a relationship because you do not want to harm your family can lead to staying in an incredibly unhappy relationship. If you currently worry more about your family than losing your partner, you need to either look for a deeper reason to stay together or start to look at the reality of what life will look like if you stay with your partner just for the family. This reasoning never works out and can often lead to highly toxic and even hostile environments, which will slowly erode the quality of your family relations, anyway. Find a substantial reason to stay together! Or decide to leave each other for good or decide to put extra effort into maintaining your relationship. At the end of the day, these are the only real options to consider.

Wanting to Maintain Your Lifestyle

Like not wanting to break apart your family, you may find out that losing your current lifestyle is a significant loss. You just enjoy your lifestyle, so much so that you fear leaving your marriage for fear of losing that lifestyle. Leaving a marriage can result in losing your home, neighborhood, the current level of financial stability, and even some of the relationships in your life. The idea of missing out on a lifestyle you have worked hard to build can seem devastating, as you may feel like you have invested too much to give up on it and lose all of that now.

If your lifestyle is the only reason you are staying, you need to consider your priorities. Is your current lifestyle truly worth coming home to unhappiness and resentment day in and day out? Think about it! In the long run, will you be happier if you maintain your lifestyle, or if you leave and give yourself a chance at building a happier life elsewhere? Don't condemn yourself to a marriage you do not love just because you are afraid of losing your lifestyle. You can always rebuild that lifestyle, or even a better one, with someone who is better suited to you, and the result will be much more magical and delightful than what you are presently living.

Religious or Cultural Beliefs

Religious or cultural beliefs can play an essential role in the decisions people make in their marriages. If you are staying in a marriage because of your religious or cultural beliefs, you have two options to consider; The first is to look for something meaningful within your relationship that makes it worth fighting for and then take the necessary actions to improve your relationship. The second is to start looking for support from people within your religion or family who can help you leave your marriage.

One of the most recurring problems people deal with when leaving a marriage is that they are often looked at differently and treated differently after. In extreme situations, you might even be shunned or shamed by your family for making this decision. It is essential that you look for as much support as possible and that you lean into that support so you can make the decision you believe is right for you and not feel alone later on. It might come with a lot of loss, but if you take the time to build up your support network, that loss will be infinitely more manageable for you to digest.

Feeling Unworthy of Better

Some people stay in unhappy relationships because they believe they will be hard-pressed to find someone better than they are already with. They might feel unworthy of being with someone better, or they might think that better people do not exist. In either scenario, you are doing yourself a disservice by reducing your self-esteem or writing off an entire group of people based on bad experiences you have had with one or a few cases in the past.

Feeling unworthy of finding someone better or believing nobody out there will give you what you truly want, can leave you in an unhappy marriage because you feel unmotivated to go and find someone better. You stay because you lack confidence in yourself, or you see your partner as sinister. If you are in a relationship where you want to stay and see improvements, lacking self-confidence or viewing your partner through evil eyes will never help. You must start to believe that you are worthy of better, and if you want to be in a better relationship with your partner, you have to start building them up and seeing them through more loving eyes. This is the only way to break through the pessimistic views and expect more optimism and happiness in your relationship and life ultimately.

You Truly Love Each Other and Feel Stuck

As I have observed in my career, both partners truly love each other and wish for nothing but a beautiful, loving life together, but they feel stuck in their current situations like Paul and Jessica who genuinely love each other from the bottom of their hearts but years of little hurts, unspoken truths, and painful experiences led to building up massive resentment, distrust, and other problems, so much so that they came to seek help from me and they have decided to work on their relationship and improve every aspect of their relationship.

Once this happens, even if you want to be in a beautiful relationship with your spouse, it may seem impossible to get past the feelings of hurt and betrayal. You may find that you think you want to leave your relationship when, in reality, you do not honestly want to go. You just feel defeated.

If you are in a situation where you love each other and have decided that you truly want to fix your relationship because you feel stuck in a position where you cannot forgive each other and move on, the fantastic news I'm going to give you is that you can heal this. Yes! Once you learn practical coping skills and apply those to your relationship, you will feel yourselves beginning to move on from your troubles and developing a new relationship that is safer and more pleasurable for both of you. So keep reading!

Chapter 4

A 7-Step Rescue Plan for Your Marriage

You may already have started to develop a deeper understanding of why your marriage is in trouble, and that's fantastic! You should not stop now, though. You must continue building momentum and using this understanding and willingness to resolve your problems to outline a solution for how you will recover your marriage so you can both start to enjoy it once again. The best solution to improve your marriage takes place over seven steps. It is designed to create a sense of safety and trust within your relationship right away and in the long term.

Understand that as you work through these seven steps, the exact approach you take and the conversations you have will depend on the fundamental causes of your unhappiness and dissatisfaction. Taking these steps in a way that is relevant to the issues you are dealing with will help you overcome them. You can always refer to these steps if different problems arise in the future, so you can fix them right away using the same powerful resolutions.

Step 1: Communication

The first and foremost step to resolving any problems regarding marriage and relationship is doubtlessly communication. Communication is often the first level of connection to fly out the door when you have issues in your marriage. You fail to effectively communicate your feelings, needs, expectations, and resolutions. Before you can do anything else, you need to rebuild your ability to communicate effectively and with an open heart.

Improving communication will require you to understand how communication works and what your roles are in conversation. It helps to rebuild dialogue around basic things first. Then, start using those skills to discuss the more challenging aspects of the issues you are going through with your partner. Once you reach this point, make sure there is a great deal of trust being infused into your relationship by being patient and compassionate with each other. You are both about to share vulnerable aspects of your feelings and concerns. Hence, this approach is crucial if you desire to have healthy and positive communication with each other.

Step 2: Conflict Resolution

Communication will naturally take you to the topic of conflict resolution. As you work through conflict resolution together, the number one goal will be to communicate in a way that is respectful and considerate of each other. You need to avoid condemning your partner or becoming angry and hurtful in the way you share since doing so will only make your partner feel defensive and create distance.

Likewise, as you listen to your partner discuss the things that have hurt them, you need to be open and compassionate about how they are feeling. Do not try to defend yourself or minimize their feelings. Instead, respect that this is how they feel and look for a way to understand why they feel this way and what made them feel this way.

As you learn to create a safe space for each other, sharing becomes more comfortable, and conflict resolution becomes more effortless. When you can trust your partner and feel safe in their presence, and when you can trust that they will work toward a solution with you, it becomes far more reasonable to see yourself moving past the issues you have been facing. This way, you can start moving toward a healthier life together, without constant resentment and blame for problems that have arisen.

Step 3: Building Trust

Trust is an essential element in any relationship, especially in marriages. When you face troubles in your marriage, it can be easy to lose trust toward your partner as you worry that they have already hurt you and so they may hurt you again. Even if they did not hurt you on purpose, you might believe that they will do it again and that regardless of the intention, the pain will still be too difficult to bear. Being hurt by our partners tends to pull more than any other type of pain because we have this expectation that our partners will always be the one to keep us safe and protect us from harm. When we realize they experience human feelings as we ourselves do, they make mistakes as we do, it can be easier to accept and navigate those feelings.

If you want to rebuild the trust in your relationship effectively, I recommend you to first understand why the offensive actions were taken in the first place. The partner who caused the hurt or betrayal needs to address their behaviors and understand them to improve their ability to communicate and have their needs met in the relationship. Likewise, the party that was hurt or betrayed needs to know how they may have played into it so they can understand their role and improve it as required. You can also work toward making new rules within your relationship that minimize the likelihood of trust being broken again. In chapter 7, we will also discuss how you can take specific actions that will show your partner that you care about them and intend to regain their trust. This way, faith is much quicker to build, and the foundation of your relationship will be more solid than ever before.

Step 4: Restoring Emotional Intimacy

Did you know that emotional intimacy will always come before physical intimacy in a marriage? Yes, that's real. Once you have begun to rebuild trust with one another, you will naturally feel yourselves beginning to feel safer with opening up on an emotional level, and you can share more emotional intimacy.

Emotional intimacy comes from more than just a physical connection. It means that you feel understood, affirmed, and cared for by your partner. In a marriage with healthy emotional intimacy, you know you can open up to your partner and talk to them about how you feel whenever you need to. They will understand and care about you and the feelings you are having. Likewise, they trust that you will communicate respectfully and always be considerate toward them.

When you can freely share your emotions and thoughts in a relationship, the relationship begins to flourish. Knowing that you share a safe space with your partner that you share with no one else unites you in a way that nothing else can. Even more than sexual intimacy, emotional intimacy will deepen your bond and allows you to feel genuinely connected to your partner.

Step 5: Rekindling Physical Passion

Emotional intimacy must come first, but physical intimacy is essential in relationships. Rekindling physical passion comes from understanding the vastness that is physical passion. Yes, you want to get back to having sex with your partner, or having more meaningful sex if your intimate relationship seems mundane or disconnected. You also want to incorporate other aspects of physical intimacy into your relationship, though. Hand holding, back rubs, hugging, cuddling, and other forms of physical affection are just as important as having sex with your partner.

Over time, physical intimacy can become challenging to maintain for many reasons. Underlying issues in the relationship, boredom, or a hectic life can lead couples to lose physical intimacy and find themselves incredibly disconnected from each other. You are learning how to rebuild that lost intimacy. One positive touch at the right time is a great way to rekindle the passion and make the fire alive again in your relationship.

Step 6: Coping With Parenting Difficulties

If you are parents, you must address any parenting difficulties you may be going through right now. Even if you are not having issues with each other as far as parenting goes, parenting can become stressful and burdensome when you are already dealing with challenges inside of your relationship. You might find that your feelings of pain and being overwhelmed bubble into the rest of your life, and this can lead you to be more grumpy or frustrated as a parent, which can result in serious parenting issues. Learning how to navigate parenting together by overcoming problems you have with each other's parenting styles and your independent parenting troubles is essential.

There are many actions you can take to help you get on the same page with your partner and increase your ability to feel supported by your partner. Knowing that you have the support and care of your partner as you navigate one of life's most challenging jobs makes a world of difference when it comes to the stress and pressure you face within your parenting experience. As you navigate these, you will likely find parenting becomes less challenging, and you have more energy and enthusiasm to enjoy a happier and healthier dynamic in your family and your marriage as well.

Step 7: Following Healthy Habits

Healthy habits are essential to any thriving relationship. Developing healthier habits allows you to step away from the habits and routines that are no longer serving your relationship so you can work to help implement strategies that will be more useful. Turning your new methods and procedures into healthy habits is a great way to ensure you are taking proper care of your relationship. This way, rather than falling into old, unhealthy habits, you can confidently rely on your new habits to help you carry the relationship forward.

As you develop newer, healthier habits, you'll also need to work toward recognizing and breaking old patterns that don't do any good to your relationship. This way, you can build a stronger connection from the foundation up, which will be much more effective in keeping your relationship going for the long haul.

Chapter 5

Communication

I firmly believe that communication is the glue of any relationship. In marriages, communication allows you to carefully and gently navigate the many challenging waters you will face as a couple. When you communicate well, navigating troubles such as hurt feelings, misunderstandings, differences of opinions, and other challenges become more natural. Communication allows you and your partner to be on the same page and *trust* you are on the same page, which results in enjoying a stronger bond and a higher level of connection and support throughout any challenges you face.

Open and honest communication should exist in every relationship, and it is something you should work toward building and reinforcing. Don't waste a day and start right away! The sooner you can rebuild this aspect of your relationship, the better. There are many steps you can take to open the channels of communication and create a safe, comfortable space for both of you to share.

How Does Communication Work?

Communication requires two people to be able to hold space for communication to occur. One person will be responsible for sharing their message, and the other will be responsible for accurately receiving that message. Once they have received the news, they need to formulate a response and feedback the first individual, who will then become responsible for accurately receiving the new information. The roles continue to reverse as each person shares their message until the conversation is over.

Many people engage in communication without thinking about what they are saying. In more heated or sensitive conversations, this can lead to more problems than solutions. Understand that each person in the conversation plays an important role, and that role must if you want to navigate the discussion effectively. When you play the part of the speaker, your job is to identify your message, decide how you will say it, consider how that message will be received, and then communicate it. On the other hand, when you are the listener, your job is to hear the news, understand what was said, determine your opinion, and develop your response. As soon as you begin to formulate your response, you switch back to the role of the speaker.

In sensitive or difficult conversations, ensure that you take each step seriously and consider what you are saying. Be aware of what you feel and think, and communicate it in a respectful and kind manner. When your partner is speaking, listen without judgment, and try to understand where they are genuinely coming from without assuming that you already know. The better you are at genuinely listening and understanding, the easier it will be to navigate these conversations.

Find the Right Time to Talk

The very first step in having healthy, open communication is finding the right time to communicate. Even casual discussion should be timed appropriately, as this will help ensure both partners are ready to give each other adequate attention to the conversation. Never underestimate the importance of casual conversation and the value it offers to your relationship.

When you are ready to communicate with your partner, whether it is casual or severe, ensure you both have the time to commit to the conversation. Actually, you must have the time and energy to contribute to the discussion as you need to be readily available for your partner during these conversations. That means you should be able to focus entirely on your partner, and you should be available to offer your emotional involvement in the discussion. This way, it feels like you have a conversation with reciprocation and positive feedback, rather than a conversation where one or both parties are not emotionally available for that conversation.

Having both partners emotionally and physically available for a conversation ensures that everything is genuinely heard and understood. This way, when you walk away from the conversation, you have both come out feeling heard, respected, received, and cherished by your partner.

Speak Face to Face

In the digital age, it can be easy to want to rely on text messages or emails to talk about important issues. These days, social skills are not incredibly sharp for the average person because we have been able to rely on digital communications for so long that the idea of involving visual emotions and physical closeness in a conversation seems intimidating. Building on a digital screen to protect you from the vulnerability in an exchange will not only save you from the exposure, but it will also prevent you from being able to convey yourself accurately. Likewise, your partner will have a hard time expressing themselves, too.

Another major issue with relying on written communication is that, more often than not, when you communicate this way, you are talking to someone who is already busy. This means they may not have enough time to read, think about, and respond to what you have said thoughtfully. This can lead to feeling as though you have been rejected or betrayed because of your partner not being able to provide you with enough attention at that moment.

Always reserve meaningful conversations for face to face communication. If you are anxious about the vulnerability aspect, work on collecting your thoughts and writing them down ahead of time so that you can see how they look and feel. Spend some time considering how you will share your thoughts, and when you are ready, you can put those into words and share them with your partner. If you feel too vulnerable or overwhelmed by the emotions, be sure to let your partner know in advance so they can take care to hold a safe space for you and make it more comfortable for you to share with them. This is an empowering way to rebuild trust in your relationship while also expanding your communication and enjoying healthier discussions.

Stay Away from Attacking Each Other

Feelings of rejection or being ignored are common when troubles arise in relationships. You may find yourself feeling so hurt by your partner that you want to attack them, coming from a place of "you hurt me, now I want you to hurt, too." You may attack your partner passively or aggressively, neither of which is an acceptable form of interacting with your partner. These attacks are a way of defending yourself and preventing further pain from occurring, yet they are also a way of holding in the problem that has already happened and blocking yourself from healing it.

When you communicate with your partner, refrain from attacking them, and ask them to refrain from attacking you, too. Use gentle, respectful tones when you are talking, and always word your sentences in a way that conveys your thoughts and feelings without trying to hurt or belittle the other person. This means no name-calling, no blaming, no shaming, and no projecting. Even passive aggressive comments can be extremely painful for your partner to receive.

The quickest way to turn these types of conversations around is to stop saying "you" and instead say "I" or "we." For example, rather than saying, "You keep rejecting me when I try to be close to you," you might say, "I feel rejected when I cuddle you, and you don't cuddle back." When you take responsibility for how you feel, it sounds as though you are sharing your experience rather than blaming your partner for how you are feeling. This prevents them from becoming defensive, so they can take a more compassionate stance and cooperate with you in resolving any problem you may be going through.

Be Honest

Total honesty in intimate relationships can be tricky. You might be afraid of hurting your partner's feelings if you tell the truth, or you might be afraid of overexposing yourself to your partner and feeling the effects of a vulnerability hangover if you share. Your partner is the one person you should be able to be completely transparent with, regardless of what you need to say. Even if it is not always easy, you should feel safe telling your partner everything relevant to your relationship.

Being honest ensures that your partner clearly understands what is happening in your mind; this way, they will not base their thoughts on what's going on solely on assumptions and guesses. Hence, the conversations take place in a careful and compassionate manner.

I must warn you that there are times when you shouldn't be one hundred percent honest with your partner, and that is when the truth would hurt them, or it will not do any good to the relationship or either of you. For example, let's say your mom says something very offensive about your spouse, and you complain to your mom that you don't like the way she talks about your partner. You might want to tell your spouse about what happened to calm yourself down or due to feeling guilty toward your spouse. But ask yourself first: is it really necessary? What benefit can it bring to my spouse and relationship? What can it give us? Of course, it gives you, your partner or your relationship nothing, but only misunderstanding, conflict and a potential fight. So, remember, not all truths should be told, especially if they are so petty and unnecessary.

Monitor Your Body Language

Your body language can send various messages to your partner. Through your body language, you can convey if you are listening and are caring toward what they are saying, or on the other hand, your body language can tell if you are distracted, defensive, put off, or disinterested in them. Your physical posture, facial expressions, level of eye contact, and actions all convey various messages to your partner.

If you want your partner to know that you are open, receptive, and engaged in a conversation, you must keep your posture open and facing them. You should also keep your facial expression soft and focused, and your eyes on your partner while they are talking. Do not take phone calls, play video games, surf the web, or become distracted in any other task while speaking with your partner. Even if you are only having a casual conversation, you need to reserve time for that kind of conversation as well. Spending at least thirty minutes a day or more, free of distractions and chatting with one another is a great way to give each other that essential quality time, so you both feel received and loved by one another.

Use the 48-Hour Rule

The 48-hour rule means that whenever your partner does something that makes you angry, you commit to telling them about it. However, you do not necessarily have to say it to them right away, especially if you are in a space where you could become defensive or offensive in the way you communicate. You might also question whether this particular subject matters that much and wonder if it will even bother you at any point in the future. Instead of rushing into a conversation about the issue that triggered your anger, give yourself 48 hours to decide whether or not you are truly upset by that particular issue, which made you angry in the first place.

After 48 hours, if you are still upset by what happened, let your partner know. You know it was big enough that it has stayed in your mind for two days. You have also had two days to think about how it has affected you and why, and to consider how you should bring it up with your spouse.

When you are ready to talk about it, ensure you don't begin to become angry toward your partner for not realizing they hurt you two days ago. Remember, you chose to hold onto it for 48 hours so you could think about it and discern if it was worth mentioning or not. This time was not to stew on it or expect your partner to figure it out, and it was time for *you* to digest the issue. Since you have decided that it is really worth discussing, you need to choose how you will communicate it positively.

After you have discussed the things that have hurt you and your partner has sincerely apologized, you must let go of whatever happened. Holding onto it or bringing it up in the future will make you bring that pain back up again, and it will only make everything worse. You need to choose to come to peace within yourself about what has happened so you can release them and come together in strength with your partner.

Communicating When You Are Angry

As I have seen in my patients, communicating when you are angry can be as tricky as you might know. It is easy to lose your traditional communication skills and rely on toxic habits like name-calling, blaming, attacking, and otherwise being cruel to your partner when you are angry. Unfortunately, while these offensive actions can give you temporary relief at that particular moment, it will cause more damage in the long run. If you are mad, you have to follow the four rules of communicating if you want to have a productive conversation with your partner. The rules are: stop, think, talk, and listen.

When you stop, give yourself a little pause. This could be a few breaths before you say anything, or it could be a break away from the conversation before you continue talking about that topic. If you need a break, commit to giving yourself some space by doing something relaxing, such as watching TV or calling a friend and putting the angry topic out of your mind. Let yourself calm down before the situation gets worse, as this will help diffuse your emotions so you can better see what is going on inside of your mind and heart.

Once your break is over, whether it was a few breaths or a few days, give yourself a moment to think. Consider what happened and what about that particular situation made you so angry and get a clear grasp of how it affected you. Ensure that you are aware of what the real problem was so that when you discuss it with your partner, you can create a resolution that fits the situation. Not clearly understanding why you got so angry initially can make you feel like you are not being fulfilled by your chosen resolutions because they are not touching down on the real challenge.

Next, you need to talk. When you speak, follow the same steps as you would in any other conversation. Ensure you both have time, talk face to face, do not engage in distractions, and be honest about what you are feeling and what you are going through. If you need to rehearse what you want to say a few times, go on and do it, so you feel more confident in sharing your thoughts. You can speak in front of a mirror to feel more motivated and confident. Otherwise, you might feel overwhelmed by the vulnerability and struggle to communicate effectively at the moment.

Lastly, you need to listen. Once you tell your partner how you feel, you need to stop talking and give them a chance to respond. Avoid hogging the conversation, and be careful not to guess their responses. Try to refrain from immediately becoming defensive only because you are afraid of being vulnerable. Allow yourself to remain open and genuinely hear what your partner has to say, as this gives you both the opportunity to express yourselves in a safe and caring environment. When you do this, navigating your angry discussions will be much useful and healthier. Following all these instructions, I explained, your resolutions will be much more fulfilling and beneficial, not only to you and your spouse but also to your relationship.

Chapter 6

Conflict Resolution

When you have reached the point where you feel that your marriage is broken, you can guarantee some conflicts have found their way in. You may even find that you and your partner experience recurring strife by way of bickering, arguing, or even full-blown fighting, and you have both agree that it feels too overwhelming and frustrating to be around each other. Arguments are for marriages, but healthy communication will provide you with a significant opportunity to fulfill the need for conflict resolution; however, that alone will not be enough to navigate particularly disturbing experiences in your relationship. In addition to healthy communication, you also need to be willing to take the necessary actions to genuinely resolve the conflict and create a safer and more pleasant environment for your marriage to prosper.

Conflict is a natural part of every healthy relationship, and every couple will inevitably experience it every now and then. Healthy conflict will occur when you disagree with, misunderstand, or have a differing set of expectations than your partner; however, it should be examined in a way where both parties feel respected, heard, understood, and fulfilled by the chosen resolution. Unhealthy conflict occurs when you disagree with, misunderstand, or have a differing set of expectations and decide that you are the only right person. Attempting to get your partner into doing everything your way, or seeing everything your way, in other words, pressuring your partner to change their mind about everything, is not helpful nor healthy. When this happens, it means that your relationship needs work, and you must change your outlook regarding what a real relationship actually is. In fact, it's a telling sign that you need to change your tactics so both of you can deal with conflict in a healthier manner.

There are seven steps to healthily navigating conflict resolution in a way that both you and your partner feel loved and respected, even when you have hit a rough patch. If you can effectively fulfill these six steps, you will be able to navigate conflict in a more beneficial manner that produces a positive and more satisfying outcome. These seven steps include unifying your primary goal, setting boundaries, finding the real issue, agreeing to disagree, compromising when you can, considering everything, and finally taking the necessary actions when you are ready.

Set a Primary Goal Together

Remember that before you even dig into conflict resolution, both of you must discuss the primary goal and talk about what you desire to come out of the conflict you are dealing with. Having a discussion beforehand about your expectations allows you to realize if you are on the same page and that you are both working toward the same objectives. Checking on this issue will save your time and energy; in addition, it immediately bridges any gaps that could otherwise make it seem like you and your partner have different goals to reach.

When couples fight and fail to realize that at the end of the day, all they want is to feel loved, wanted, and respected, they might feel a lack of support. This feeling of the void can make you fight even more fiercely because you think the person who is supposed to be on your side is instead fighting against you and wants to hurt you. This misunderstanding could potentially make an already vulnerable situation feel even more painful and expose you to more challenges regarding resolving the conflict.

Some excellent common goals you might share would be to create a space where you are both respected, loved, and cared for. In such a beautiful and peaceful space, you will feel supported by each other, and resolving the issues will seem easier and more achievable. Interestingly, when you set goals to achieve a win-win situation, it looks more simple to cope with the conflicts, and both of you will act with more motivation and a stronger sense of responsibility.

Set Boundaries

After setting your primary goal, it's time to set boundaries. I want to make this clear for once and all that even during a heated argument, everyone deserves to be treated with respect and thoughtfulness; that's why we need to set boundaries. Let me assure you that it's your absolute right to let your partner know that you will not tolerate being cursed at, called names, or treated disrespectfully. If they begin acting like this, choose to walk away from the argument temporarily and agree to come back at it at a later time, when your partner promises to go on with mutual respect.

Boundaries may be challenging to assert, especially when you are angry, and you feel as though you need to defend yourself. If you are feeling hurt by what your partner is doing, you might even find yourself wanting to retaliate and push back at your partner so you can hurt them too. However, retaliation and crossing each other's boundaries are not productive; plus that, they will not allow you both to get to the bottom of your problems together. The only possible way which helps you go forward and make improvements with the conflicts is through mutual respect, understanding and compassion.

Find the Real Issue

Conflict often worsens when one or both partners feels they are arguing for a different purpose. Fighting for different objectives creates some sort of detachment between partners. For example, let's say you are angry because your partner did not consider you before committing to significant plans, so now you feel left out. On the surface, this argument may seem as though it is about the plans made, but for you, it could be about the fact that you were not included in the decision making, which ultimately indicates to you that your presence and your opinions are not appreciated and honored. However, your partner might not realize that this is how you are genuinely feeling, and they may misunderstand your real feelings and imagine that the issue is the plan itself.

If you are unaware of what the real issue is for you at that moment, you can either ask to have some space so you can think about it or talk it over with your partner and try to understand it together. In most cases, arguments are not really about what has happened, but how it made a partner feel upset and hurt. You might not feel valued, respected, wanted, cherished, prioritized, thought about, loved, or held in high esteem in your relationship based on the actions someone has chosen to take. Feeling this way, of course, is painful, and it becomes even more challenging when both partners start to feel this way.

Once you have found the real issue behind the sadness one or both of you are feeling, you need to stop focusing so much on the action and instead focus on the way the hurt partner is feeling. Discuss the experience to understand why it created that feeling in the first place, but also be open to discussing other reasons which caused that feeling too. The better you both understand the primary source of those disturbing feelings, the easier it will be to find a solution to stop having this problem.

Agree to Disagree

Let me assure you that all couples in the world disagree on some issues, so I invite you to calm down and remember that, in your relationship too, there will be issues you and your partner disagree on. You will not always be of like mind about everything. That being said, it's evident that sometimes you'll naturally have arguments, as each partner wants to prove why their opinion is right and why the other partner needs to change their mind. This behavior just leads to the ongoing conflict that probably won't ever have a resolution since neither party is willing to change their mind, and each one thinks she/he is right. If you and your partner cannot find an answer to an issue, you need to drop it for now.

In order not to be stuck on a petty issue, try to focus on what matters the most, and accept the fact that you, as a couple, can move forward without agreeing on every single thing. On the other hand, if you are dealing with an issue that cannot be dropped or put aside, for now, I suggest you take a break, have your space, think about it and come back later to the issue. This way, you can go back together with a clearer mind and a more significant ability to negotiate the outcome. During your break, you may have even discovered alternate solutions or options that you did not know existed, some of which may offer the perfect solution for what you are looking for.

If you realize that you and your partner disagree on fundamental issues and that you cannot reasonably drop it, it may be because you and your partner are incompatible. For example, if you want children and they don't, if you want to get married and they don't, or if you want to live in a particular town and they don't, chances are you'll go your separate ways or that your relationship wouldn't work well in the long run. While it is possible to compromise on things, these types of fundamental issues are often challenging to compromise on and often lead to one or both parties being unhappy with what they have settled for.

Compromise When You Can

Compromising can be an incredibly challenging thing to do, but it is an essential part of finding a resolution for your issues. Whenever you can, look for a compromise that allows you to feel represented and satisfied by the solution you have found to the problem you are facing. A real and fair compromise should allow both of you to feel as though you are walking away from a conflict with something positive in hand. It should never result in one person compromising and achieving all of their goals, and one person compromising and not getting any of the objectives they wanted to reach after compromising. The goals achieved by each partner should more or less be equal, and both partners should still walk away with what they want. This way, you are confident that you both feel represented and respected by the resolution you have come up with.

In some situations, you might not be able to make a fair compromise since certain circumstances make it impossible, and this can give you a hard time finding the right solution. In this case, I invite you to look at the bigger picture and ensure that your negotiations always result in equality on the whole. This way, if one person is not getting close to what they wanted in this isolated situation, they know that they are still valued and included. The primary key here is to be cautious about imbalance and inequality. Be careful that is one partner is not repeatedly getting the short end of the stick while the other person gets what they exactly want every single time.

When you are compromising with your partner, remember that your primary goal is reaching a win-win situation every time. You do not want to compete with your partner or come out the winner because, in doing so, your partner comes out the loser, and at the end of the day, you both lose in the long run, and what you lose is obviously the special relationship you've built together. Always make sure that, overall, both partners are being adequately represented and are satisfied with the outcomes. If it is not possible, work together on resolving the disturbing feeling of the partner who feels that they have lost out on something they were looking forward to from the compromise.

Consider Everything

Conflict can be all-consuming, and the feelings that arise as a result can make you feel as though nothing else in life matters except this conflict right here, right now. Conflicts can range from being so fundamental and so petty. For instance, if you are conflicted about whether or not you should have children because one partner wants children and the other doesn't, then it is fair for this to be an all-consuming conflict as it genuinely could signal the existence of some fundamental issues or differences that need to be discussed to see if you can solve them or you should go your separate ways. If, however, you are conflicted because one partner wants Thai food and the other is craving Mexican food for dinner, this is obviously too trivial to be worthy of being an all-consuming conflict. This is something that can easily be worked out and is certainly not worth breaking up over.

When you face conflict, any kind of conflict, always pause, step back, and try to see the bigger picture. Now, is the issue *really* worth arguing over? And, if it is, is it worth breaking up over? If not, you need to tone it down and start engaging in a healthier conflict resolution solely based on the fact that this argument is not worth the time and energy.

What I suggest to my patients who go through conflicts every now and then in their marriage is to pause, step back and consider everything from their partner's perspective, and look at what is causing their partner to feel the way they feel. Then, examine their emotional response, what they are saying, and how they are behaving. Do they usually behave this way? Or does this particular behavior seem unusual to them? Are they generally good at compromising, or do they tend to become passive or dominant in compromising? Consider where they are coming from and allow that to help you decide how to navigate the situation. The more compassion you have for each other, the more you empathize with each other, the more you feel each other's feelings and the more you are familiar with each other's mindset, the easier it will get for the two of you to move on from your problems.

Make the Necessary Changes

Finally, you must follow through on any of the changes you have committed to making together. Once you have settled on a resolution and agreed to disagree, compromised, and finally come up with how you will move forward, you have to take the next step, which is changing some little things for the good of your relationship. Not taking immediate action on those changes and putting them on the back burner will make your partner believe that you did not take them seriously; in fact, it will make them feel as though you are willing to discuss problems and become aware of the solutions, but you do not value your partner or relationship enough to make those changes. This is incredibly unhealthy for your relationship and will consequently create more hurt and make the situation even more complicated than ever before.

Naturally, it may take some practice to get to that point, but it should not seem as though absolutely nothing is happening. If zero action is being taken on the intended resolution, your resolution won't function, and you will find yourself in more complicated conflicts. What you can do is showing your partner that you do value them and that you care about them by taking action on the intended resolution and that you are willing to put the effort in.

After you have followed through on your intended changes, I advise you to take the time to talk with your partner and discuss how the resolution is feeling for each of you. This follow-up conversation will allow you to determine if your solution is enough or if more changes need to be made for the conflict to be resolved. Regular communication around this will verify that your dispute is genuinely resolved in a healthy, positive manner. This way, the conflict does not become an issue for you again in the future because it has been resolved to full closure.

Chapter 7

Building Trust

I've often noticed that there is a common misconception among couples that says: unless something blatantly obvious has sabotaged the trust in your marriage, that trust will never be broken. Let me be clear about it and tell you that the reality is something different; while more significant problems like betrayals or infidelity can lead to broken trust, so can smaller and less obvious acts, such as not listening to your partner or telling little white lies. Even if one partner feels repeatedly rejected by their spouse in seemingly minor ways, it can make that partner feel a lack of trust in their spouse. If you are at the point where you are facing troubles in your marriage, you can guarantee that there has been some sort of destruction in the trust in your marriage.

Why Is Trust So Important to a Marriage?

It goes without saying that trust is essential to a marriage; since marriage is a relationship where you share more emotional, mental, and physical overlap than you do in nearly any other relationship in your life. In a marriage, you and your partner agree to live your lives together, which includes sharing intimate, meaningful connections with your partner in many different ways. From living together in the same house to raising a family (or not) or deciding on how you will structure your lifestyle, overall, there are many decisions that must be made together. You must have a significant amount of trust in your partner to know that they will make these decisions using similar values as you do, and with consideration to you and your needs, too. Both of you cannot independently make choices that affect your shared life because this could lead to one partner not being adequately represented by the choices being made. All choices should, ideally, provide both of you with the opportunity to feel satisfied with the life you are building together.

In contrast, when there is a lack of trust in your marriage, every aspect of your life can start to feel unstable and uncertain. For instance, your spouse seems no longer the person you could totally trust and confide in. Even if it's not true, and it's only the impression you get, it can still *feel* true, and that feeling can make your relationship feel like an unsafe place to be. As soon as your marriage starts to feel unsafe, everything will feel unsafe and confusing, as a natural consequence. That, compounded by the feeling of being out of sync with or betrayed by your partner, can create serious hurt feelings, making everything feel even more painful and gut-wrenching.

Trust is essential to a marriage because it provides a sense of stability, connection, and safety for both you and your partner. When you trust your partner, you know that they will be considerate of you, they will respect you, and they will cherish you. You know that you never have to worry about them harming you or doing something damaging to you and your relationship because you can totally trust them to protect your relationship, just as you would. Also, the trust allows both of you to experience intimacy on a physical as well as emotional level; sharing your thoughts and worries, making love, and cuddling are the proofs. When you fully trust that your partner is in your corner and on your side, your marriage feels as solid as a rock and operates from a solid foundation, enabling both of you to relish a more enriching relationship.

The Unexpected Ways Showing that Trust Is Broken

Trust can be broken in many ways, ranging from major and obvious to smaller and inconspicuous ones. Primary ways by which trust can be broken in a relationship include infidelity, betrayal, significant lies about finances or personal history, and other big issues. These problems are often extremely shocking for the victimized partner to learn about, and they can create a serious and massive rift in your relationship with your partner. If you are the offender, you have shattered your partner's illusion of the happy, trusting marriage that you have been upholding with them while secretly betraying them for some period of time. If you are the victim, you may have just had your entire reality blown up by your partner as you realize that they have been lying to you and begin to wonder if anything you ever shared together was real.

Outside of obvious betrayals, though, there are many other ways that marriages lose trust over time. This can happen for one or both partners, accumulating over time and leading to even more severe issues. For example, let's say that your partner never seems to value your time together but shows it in minimal ways. Perhaps you plan for date nights, and every time they end up working later at the office, and you have to postpone your date together. Although you do go, the constant need to postpone your dates leads to you feeling as though your partner does not value you or cherish you, and so you stop trusting them because every time they claim that they do, in fact, value and cherish you, you cannot believe them. Their actions and their words do not align, and so you lose trust.

Trust can be lost in these seemingly minor ways through many different instances of minor discrepancies between what someone says and what someone does. Anytime your words and actions do not align, especially if it happens on a continual basis, it can lead to a disruption of the trust between you and your partner. That does not just hurt feelings, it breaks trust, and that broken trust damages the very foundation of the relationship. Repeat offenses against your shared trust from your partner results in broken trust, and eventually, that broken trust leads to damaged relationships and divorces. That is not a possibility; that is the inevitable fate of a relationship with no trust. You must take this lack of trust seriously, even if it was developed from seemingly small situations because they can and will sabotage your relationship every single time.

The Necessary Steps for Rebuilding Trust

Rebuilding trust is a process, and both partners must be ready to commit to that process if they really want to see improvements in their relationship. If these steps are not taken, you will not successfully correct the fatal errors you have made over time. At times, rebuilding trust can take weeks, months, or even years because the damage has been so massive that it takes time for both partners to feel fully secure within the relationship once again. As long as both partners remain committed to the idea of repairing the relationship, however, changes can be made, and both can hope for a brighter future together.

Aside from patience, you must be ready to understand your partner, even if you do not entirely agree with them. You need to create a sense of awareness around where they are coming from and compassion around why they have the feelings they do. The more you come to understand why your partner feels how they do and how you have contributed to their feelings, the easier it will be for you to create positive changes in your relationship. Through this understanding, you make the changes they need, rather than the changes you believe will help.

It is also essential that both you and your partner have the opportunity to express and release the anger that you feel caused by the betrayals you have experienced. When your trust with your partner has been broken, you can start to feel a great deal of anger and frustration grow, and you may even begin to resent your partner. Respectfully expressing and completely releasing this anger must happen if you will fully restore the trust between yourself and your partner. Failure to fully express and release this anger can decrease your level of trust in your partner. Even though you are making efforts to make things work out, that unexpressed anger creates a vicious circle situation.

Lastly, you need to provide your partner with tangible proofs that you are working toward rebuilding the trust based on the actions you are taking. Through practical, healthy steps to rebuild trust, your partner will begin to realize that they can trust you, and this will make breaking through the emotional and mental barriers much easier. If your partner cannot see those tangible proofs and that change is actually happening, they will not be able to rebuild trust in your marriage because you will still be acting in a way that cultivates a lack of trust. Once you have taken all of these steps, the trust will begin to come back.

Create a Sense of Understanding Between You Two

Even in seemingly clear-cut cases of betrayal, there are always two sides and two viewpoints to every story. It is important that the person who sabotaged the trust be upfront and honest about what they have done, and why they have done that, and that they provide clear answers to every question their partner needs to get answered. The more transparent this partner can be, and the more compassionate and patient they are with the process, the easier it will be for the betrayed party to understand the situation clearly and precisely. It is important that the offending party take all responsibility for their actions while being clear about what was going on within the relationship or within themselves, which lead to those actions being taken.

If there was a problem within the relationship that led to their betrayal, the offending partner should not become defensive or accuse the betrayed partner of what happened. Instead, they should clearly explain in a gentle and compassionate manner, as defensiveness and accusations will only create more significant problems at this point. Even if the betrayed party has initially been the root cause of the problem, following a betrayal is not the time to start blaming them as this will deepen the gap and exacerbate the problems.

The offending party should seek to understand the betrayed party, as well, as the betrayed party will be experiencing their own unique situation, too. The better both parties can understand each other, the easier it will be for them to have compassion for where the other person is coming from and to feel confident that the other party wants to move on from the conflicts and proceed in the marriage. When one or both partners close off or isolate themselves at this point, it can create a giant crack in the marriage. Therefore, it is crucial that you do everything you can to overcome the betrayal, even if it feels impossible. Remember that doing it together is the only way to get through it.

Release All of the Anger You Are Feeling

Of course, I can empathize with you; being betrayed by your partner can be extremely devastating and painful. We have all experienced it at one time or another and have felt how distressing it can be to know that your partner, who you love and trust the most, has the ability to hurt you so deeply. Believing that they *have* hurt you so deeply is a hard pill to swallow and can create extreme feelings of anger as you start to resent your partner for treating you in such a way. However, if you want to get through the betrayal, rebuild trust, and be able to move on, you need to be willing to release all of the anger you are feeling and come together in a more positive manner.

Understand that releasing the anger you feel does not have to be a leap decision, nor does it have to be something that happens all at once. It may take time, and you may need to have as many conversations as necessary to be able to fully understand the anger you are experiencing and to respectfully express it to your partner, then fully release it. As you continue to have these conversations and develop the willingness to release your anger, you will find yourself starting to let go completely.

Once you have had the conversation and agreed to release the anger, you should do everything within your power to let it go. Do not insist on bringing these points up in arguments or holding them against your partner, as doing so will only give you reasons to continue feeling hurt by your partner. This kind of behavior will not give you a feeling of total relief from the anger nor an ability to rebuild trust with your partner.

Provide Evidence of Your Commitment

Evidence of your commitment is vital in your marriage, especially when it comes to rebuilding trust. It is true that you should never test your partner as you will always be holding them in contempt and putting a strain on your relationship. However, the evidence must be provided when it comes to something so crucial as rebuilding trust. Without evidence, the betrayed party won't have access to a way of knowing or trusting that changes are being made; in other words, there won't be any visible proof to rely on in order to break through the walls of betrayal and move back into a space of trust.

Evidence of your commitment to rebuilding trust is as simple as proving that you will do what you say you will do. This is true for everything you say you will do, no matter how small it is or how irrelevant it might be to the original betrayal. Once someone has had their trust broken, they will be especially cautious of all of their feelings and doing everything they can to avoid having their trust shattered again in any other way. This means that if you broke the trust of your partner through infidelity, that trust will further be broken again by not showing up on time to your commitments, not keeping in touch with them, or otherwise not being congruent in your actions. You must rebuild trust in every possible way if your partner can succeed to fully trust you again.

The more evidence you can provide to your partner about your commitment to rebuilding trust, the more your partner will believe you and be able to trust you again. It is imperative that you take action on this immediately and that you continue to do so on a daily basis if you want things to work out again. It will take a great deal of evidence to prove that change has happened, as even one minor setback can deepen the already painful wound your partner is experiencing from the broken trust.

Rebuild Trust Through Practical Steps

Once you have reached this point, you are ready to start taking practical steps to rebuild trust in your marriage. There are steps that must be taken by the offender, as well as the betrayed, to create a sense of trust in your marriage once again. If your marriage has been going through some serious problems for any period, I want to assure you that both you and your partner have done things to damage the trust in your marriage, meaning you are both the offender and the betrayed. In this case, you need to take all necessary steps to work on rebuilding trust from both angles, depending on what situation you are focusing on in each moment. Be graceful in understanding that you are both hurting, and you have both hurt the other person, so you must both take equal action to improve the relationship between yourself and your partner.

For the offender, you need to show that you are a better person and that you want to improve your marriage by drastically changing your disturbing behavior. You will do this by considering which behaviors have led to the shattering of your partner's trust and then change them. The changes you make should be visible in your manners and should be discussed with your partner ahead of time so that they know what you are doing and what changes are being made to reflect your transformation.

In addition to making obvious changes, you need to be honest and take responsibility for your errors. Once you have been caught in an act of betrayal, whatever it may be, total transparency is essential if you desire to regain your partner's trust. Most probably, your partner will have questions about the betrayal and your motivations behind it. In this step, total honesty and transparency are crucial; remember that you cannot, and you shouldn't lie, even about the smallest things regarding the issue. Even if you think the answers will be disturbing to your partner or uncomfortable for you to admit to, you need to be honest with your partner if you really hope for recovery and moving on. You also need to take full responsibility and own the actions you took, regardless of why you took them or what lead you to behave that way. At the end of the day, *you* chose to behave that way; no one else forced you. Your choice for how you handled a situation hurt your partner, and you are the one who must take ownership of those behaviors. Trying to blame your partner, or anyone else, for their actions or any role they may have played leading up to your decision is unfair and immature and can even block the way of recovery and rehabilitation.

If you are the one who was betrayed, you as well have work to do. Although it was not your fault that the hurtful actions were taken, it is your responsibility to contribute to the resolution if you want your relationship to be recovered. You can contribute to the resolution by working on understanding why the betrayal occurred in the first place and how you can act now. Understanding why it all took place <u>*does not*</u> mean you have to take responsibility for what your partner did; that is their own responsibility and is solely their fault. However, if they made that choice because they were unhappy within the relationship, you need to work toward understanding why they were unhappy and what can be done in order to improve your marriage from now on.

Once you have committed to giving your partner a second chance, you need to be committed to helping make the relationship better, and that includes providing positive responses every time your partner does what you want them to do. It is not helpful to be angry, resentful, or aggressive toward your partner as this will only worsen the relationship further. You both need to work toward making a more positive, loving environment for the two of you to enjoy the time you spend with each other. Positive reinforcement will help you advocate for the changes you need while also creating a more sustainable environment for your partner and recovering from the troubles your relationship was facing before, during, and after the betrayal.

If you were betrayed, it is essential to know that you are entirely at liberty to decide. If you do not want to continue the relationship any further, it's your choice, and your partner and people around you must understand and respect your decision. After you have considered the steps for rebuilding trust, or even put effort into rebuilding trust with your partner, if you decide that it is not working for you, it is okay to change your mind or decide to end things. Just be honest with yourself and your partner.

While each one of you has independent work to do when it comes to rebuilding trust, it is important to understand that this work needs to be done together. This means you need to have open, honest communication between you and your partner on an ongoing basis so you can continue to discuss how the changes are supporting your marriage, how you are feeling, and what needs to happen in order for things to continue getting better. The more you have these honest discussions, the easier it will be to recover the trust in your relationship.

Chapter 8

Restoring Emotional Intimacy

As you begin to rebuild the trust in your relationship, you will discover that emotional intimacy follows naturally as the next step. In my opinion, emotional intimacy is an essential element in any marriage; it is the glue that bonds you together through thick and thin. It is often said that among all people in the world, your partner should be the one that you can talk to about everything, and you should feel safe going to them with all of your thoughts and emotions. This truly means *all* of them.

Often, couples who are facing hardships lose their emotional intimacy because they stop trusting each other and start to feel disconnected from each other. The changes in their relationship can make emotional intimacy fall apart because they stop feeling safe for coming to each other and talking about everything they need to share with each other. Instead, they start closing off certain parts of themselves or hiding parts of themselves for fear of being judged, ill-received, or ignored for the way they are feeling. This is not how it should be with your partner.

Emotional Intimacy is the Foundation

Emotional intimacy is the element that makes a marriage stand out from all other types of relationships. While friendships and familial relationships do rely on a certain level of emotional vulnerability to exist in order for those relationships to thrive, nothing compares to the emotional intimacy experienced in a marriage. When that emotional intimacy is cut off, so is the foundation of the entire relationship. What follows is a rapid deterioration of the relationship as it moves from a real marriage to a simple roommate-type relationship for both partners. Instead of feeling that you and your partner share something special, intimate, and unique, you feel as though you are sharing a house and a life but lacking the energy of a real marriage.

In a marriage, emotional intimacy allows you to be your true, unfiltered self in front of your partner in virtually every possible way. It's the emotional intimacy that makes you feel safe and comfortable in your ability to express yourself, your thoughts, and your feelings in front of your partner without fear of being judged or punished for the way you are, think or feel. You know that you can communicate your desires and passions, as well as your fears and deepest regrets and that your partner will respect you and continue to love you and hold you in high esteem no matter what.

As you build this level of security and reliability together, you create the opportunity for a stronger bond to manifest. Through this, you begin to experience that deep, magnetic attraction and connection that marriages are well-known for.

Turning Off the Electronics

One of the quickest ways to start rebuilding emotional intimacy in your marriage is to turn off the electronics, or at least silence them. Distractions have always been an obstacle for emotional intimacy to flourish, and in our modern world, the distractions are exaggerated through the biggest mania, which, undoubtedly, is electronics. Cell phones, computers, tablets, video game consoles, and televisions can all pose a distraction by causing both you and your partner to be more focused on the virtual world and its false appeal rather than each other. Although you may be sitting with each other or spending time together, it is not the same because you are not spending time *with* each other; you are spending time *near* each other. This can create the illusion that you spend a lot of time together when, in reality, the energy is not being shared with each other but invested in your electronics instead.

Turning off or silencing your electronics allows you to start enjoying more quality time with your partner by encouraging you to focus your energy on each other rather than on those distractions. This means that you can start engaging in real, meaningful conversations in which you communicate about important things, or even just stare into each other's eyes and cuddling each other without distractions. As you turn these devices off, you also encourage yourselves to communicate about the more challenging things face to face, rather than through a screen. In our modern world, many couples refuge in texting or emailing each other about the problems they are going through rather than talking face to face, which can significantly inhibit emotional intimacy. When this happens, what you are essentially saying is that you do not feel emotionally safe or supported enough to talk about the more sophisticated things with your partner. And, rather than trying, you hide behind a screen to say it instead. Written communication can be helpful with getting the ball rolling, but it needs to be a number one priority for you to start moving all significant conversations over to face to face communication. This means both positive and challenging communications should be shared in person, rather than being hidden behind a text message.

Creating a Sense of Emotional Availability

Generating emotional availability for your partner can seem challenging, as you might wonder what this even means or how you can generate emotional availability to begin with. Emotional availability is generated through being ready, willing, and able to talk to your partner about whatever they need to talk about, without feeling hostile or defensive about what is being said. If you immediately start defending yourself or blaming your partner or anyone else about the way they are feeling or what is being said, you are creating an inhospitable environment and effectively sabotaging your emotional intimacy.

Instead of listening in order to defend and protect yourself from your partner, you need to drop your guard and learn how to listen with compassion and curiosity. Seek to understand why your partner feels the way they do and look for opportunities to consider how they may have reached the point of feeling this way. Rather than taking everything they say personally, take it as information being shared with the intention of helping you find a way to make your relationship more enjoyable and enriching for both of you. When you change your attitude, it is easier to remember that you and your partner want the same thing, and therefore you need to get on the same page through empathy and compassion, rather than defensiveness and hostility.

Increasing the Time You Spend Together

Spending more time with your partner is a wonderful way to rebuild the emotional intimacy in your relationship, as it gives you time to get to know each other once again. After any significant amount of time together, it can be easy to feel like you know everything there is to know about your partner. Unfortunately, this perspective can give you a false image of your relationship while also sabotaging it because you behave as though you know everything there is to know, while, in reality, you don't. People grow and change on a daily basis. You are not the same person you were last year, last month, or even yesterday; that's why spending time with your partner is the only way to continue learning about who your partner is and who they are becoming over time. Moreover, this allows you to discover their new interests, understand what is going on in their day to day life, and develop a sense of connection with them and their ever-changing opinions and mannerisms.

The more time you spend with your partner, the more you develop a deep sense of connection with them. You recognize the way they move, the words they use, and the expressions they have for each emotion, thought, or experience. As you continue to spend more time with your partner, you realize that they are an incredibly unique individual and that every day they are changing and growing into an even more impressive person. Ultimately, you'll gain the opportunity to fall in love with your partner all over again.

While you spend time together, be sure to regularly ask the question, "How can I support you?" Open up room for conversation about the intimate goings-on of your lives and truly listen to your partner. See if there are ways that you can support or encourage them in their endeavors, and do everything you can to uplift them in any possible way, whether that is standing back and cheering them up or taking on an active role in something they are doing.

It can be easy to take advantage of your time together when you have been in a committed relationship for a lengthy period. It can also be easy to let the amount of time you spend together fade as you both become absorbed with your careers, family life, friends, hobbies, and other commitments you have in your lives. Remember, it is not enough to just see each other for a few minutes each morning, and each evening, you need to dedicate time specifically to you and your partner to be together and enjoy each other's company. The more you do this, the more connected you will feel, and the more you will be able to mutually nourish the relationship you are sharing, thus deepening your emotional intimacy.

Striking a Balance Between the Individual and the Couple

When emotional intimacy has taken a nosedive in any relationship, it is not uncommon for two extremely different roles to spring out of that: the chaser and the runner. The chaser will be the partner who recognizes emotional intimacy has begun to fall apart and who starts chasing their partner in an effort to bring that connection back together. They may routinely point out that emotional intimacy has faltered, force their partner into spending time with them and criticize themselves, their partner, and the relationship for what is going on. At first, it may be innocent and relatively harmless, though over time, it can become more harmful and sabotaging as the individual becomes desperate to restore intimacy in their relationship.

Meanwhile, the runner is the one who sees the emotional intimacy faltering and either denies it or runs away for fear of having to deal with the level of vulnerability that is required to repair such a connection. They find themselves anxious about what has happened and also wanting to repair the damage, though they begin to feel driven away and overwhelmed by the desperate actions of their partner. Rather than feeling supported and encouraged to come back together, they feel as though they are being driven away.

As you repair emotional intimacy, attempting to do it all at once can actually feed into this unhealthy pattern. The chaser may begin to use this as evidence that they need to try harder, while the runner may begin to feel even more suffocated and struggle to identify how to connect in a less overwhelming manner. Rather than trying to recover all of your emotional intimacy in one go, you need to step back and evaluate the importance of the individual and the couple. This means you need to give each other space to be independent in order to come back together with more enthusiasm and passion. During both independence and togetherness, both partners should be looking to heal from the ailments that have led to the disconnect so that they can start coming back together if that is their mutual goal. Alone, they should be seeking to refill their personal cup, improve their emotional and mental health, rebuild the joy in their lives, and gain perspective around their relationship with their partner. Together, they should able to do the same things they can do on their own while sharing the goal of learning healthier ways of rebuilding emotional intimacy together.

When a balance is created between the individual and the couple, both partners will be able to comfortably fulfill their needs of drawing their partner closer while having their personal space, which is a strategy that makes you become two healthier individuals in the end. The healthier you and your partner are independently, the healthier you will be within your relationship, and the stronger your marriage will grow. It may feel counterintuitive to set aside independent time and couple time intentionally, but only in doing so you can massively improve the health and quality of your marriage.

Creating a "Fun List"

Marriages often find their way of becoming routine and mundane over time. While it doesn't happen willfully, you gradually become used to spending every day together, and it is only natural for you to fall into routines and fixed schedules. Even time spent together may lack the spark it once had, as you do the same thing every time, making it feel that your time together is not as unique as it once was. Perhaps you eat in the same restaurants, watch the same types of movies with the same snacks, go to the same places, or generally go through the same motions every time you have time together with your partner.

Everybody wants to do the things they love, even if they are routine, but you should know that bringing more spice, fun and spontaneity into your marriage only benefits your marriage. Having fun together by doing new, vibrant, exciting things is a great way to experience great joy and euphoria with your partner. When you share those feelings with each other, it not only deepens your emotional connection but also strengthens your emotional intimacy.

If you have been having a particularly troublesome time with your partner, it might be helpful to start having some real fun together. Then, after a day of laughing, having fun, and genuinely enjoying each other, you can come back together and try to discuss the way you feel and the troubles you are dealing with in your marriage. By doing so, you can overcome the constant feeling of doom and hurt feelings, and also remind yourselves why you love each other and love spending your life together, and that's why you are encouraged to look for solutions, rather than fixate on the problems. So try to see things in the bigger picture!

Further, the amplified sense of emotional connection you developed during your fun time can also help increase your compassion for your partner, making it easier for you to genuinely look at things from their perspective and have a complete outlook of the relationship.

A great way to boost pleasure and cheerfulness in your marriage is by making a "fun list." A fun list is a list of enjoyable and fun activities you can do with your partner. Pick items from the list frequently, and whether you are in a good mood or not, use it as an opportunity to come closer together. If you find yourself struggling with arguments, purposefully do something from that list *first*, then discuss your troubles second. This method is highly effective in bringing you closer together and helping you navigate your problems in a more constructive, as well as a friendly manner.

Talking Through the Important Things

Nothing will increase your emotional intimacy with your partner more than talking will. Taking the time to communicate about the valuable things in a face to face manner will play a primary role in helping you connect with your partner on a more profound level. Don't limit yourself! I suggest you talk about everything from your dreams and hopes in life to how you want to spend your next summer or what you want to do with your mutual savings account. Develop goals that you can work toward together, and talk about them frequently so you can learn to build things as a team and grow through any challenges you may encounter along the way.

As you talk, practice communicating your wants and needs frankly while also actively listening to your partner so you can understand what they are communicating back to you. This is a perfect opportunity to grow together and practice sharing in an honest, vulnerable, and emotional manner. That way, when it comes to more complex topics, you already feel comfortable talking about them with your partner and are able to manage the discussion more effectively and more skillfully.

CHAPTER 9

Rekindling the Spark

You may have heard that sexual intimacy is vital to a healthy, thriving marriage. Various studies argue about how much sex you should be having and how important sex is, but all studies agree that on one level or another, sex and physical intimacy is fundamental to marriage. As for emotional intimacy, sexual intimacy is something you share exclusively with your partner. When this physical intimacy is lacking or disappears altogether, it can eliminate the sensation of emotional connection as well. You begin to feel like roommates or friends since one of the major elements that make your relationship more distinctive than your relationship with anyone else is absent.

Here I want you to know that rekindling the passion is surprisingly challenging and needs so much work once it has been eliminated from a relationship, but it can certainly be done if you follow the instructions that I provide in this chapter precisely. But before, let's see together what keeps the fire from reigniting!

Standing in the way of rekindling the passion may be feelings of betrayal and disappointment, a lack of trust, or even a feeling of awkwardness and embarrassment. However, you are here to overcome all those possible obstacles and learn to enjoy each other's physical intimacy once again.

As I have observed so many couples during the years of my experience as a therapist, it is not uncommon to lose physical intimacy, but once it's disappeared for a certain amount of time, the partners start to feel uncomfortable with being naked or physically intimate with each other, based mainly on the simple fact that you have not engaged this way in a long time. Unlike those times when you first got together, and there was an insatiable thirst for getting physical with each other, now there are solely hurt feelings, making it all feel less exciting and more intimidating than anything else. If you feel any of these feelings with your partner, I want you to know that what you are feeling is just natural, normal and human and can be entirely resolved. For sure, it will take time, effort, and commitment, just like any other aspect of healing your marriage, but it can be completely reversed, and you will undoubtedly enjoy a stronger and healthier sex life once more.

Why You Need Sex in Your Marriage

As I mentioned previously, sex is the most intimate physical act you share with another human, and it is something that we want to reserve exclusively for our partner in our marriage. When you connect with your partner sexually, you experience a deepened sense of physical, emotional and even spiritual intimacy. The experience of sharing orgasms together also helps wire the brain for romance and love by releasing oxytocin in your brain. Oxytocin is the feel-good love and bonding hormone, and when it is produced more frequently, you start to feel a more profound sense of connection with your partner on a biological level.

Dry spells are a normal part of any marriage and relationship, but when sex is lacking in your marriage for a very long period of time, you start to lose sight of the special connection you share and find yourself feeling as though there is something missing between you and your partner. That is because there is an intimate connection driven by a sexual relationship.

Dedicating some time to maintain your sex life alive is beneficial and essential for healthy and vibrant sex life. It is often called 'maintenance sex,' meaning that you have sex just to have it, even if you don't feel like it at that moment. It requires you and your partner to routinely set aside time for each other and work toward making it passionate, intimate, and unforgettable. The so-called 'maintenance sex' should not always be a routine romp in the sheets before bed or on a specific day when the kids are away from home. Make time for spontaneous sex, role-playing, and other sexual games with each other, as this will help you take out the mundane aspect of a routine and turn your sex into something exciting and pleasurable.

Making Time for Sexual Intimacy

Scheduled sex may not precisely refer to passionate sex, and for many couples putting it on the schedule actually makes having sex at that time even more challenging as it feels obligatory and forced. Rather than trying to determine a fixed time for when you will have sex, make a point to have sex with your partner, and actually make time in your schedule for it. When you place the intention of having sex at the forefront of your mind, it becomes easier to find a few times per week that you can enjoy sex with each other. It can be as few as one or as many as daily or even more, so long as it feels right for both of you. The idea is to set the intention to make time and then to take advantage of that time when you find it.

Avoid talking yourself out of making use of that time or pressuring yourself to make it extra special in any way. Instead, just focus on making that time about being together with your partner and sharing some sort of intimacy together. If it is not possible to have full intercourse at that moment, either because you do not have the time or because you feel too uncomfortable after such a long period without it, try to make love in other ways. Sometimes, extended periods without sex can make it too uneasy for one or both partners, so it may feel more comfortable to start with a sensual back rub or a cuddle in the bed, either partially or entirely nude. These steps are all excellent in helping bring you and your partner closer together and recreate that lost special physical bond.

Communication and Copulation

Communication plays an essential role in every step of rebuilding your marriage, and it is no different when it comes to rekindling the spark. Having sex with your partner is not just about the physical acts of penetration, but about the process of connecting with each other on a physical level. Invest time in asking your partner about how they feel, what they like, and how you can help them feel more secure and comfortable while you are having sex. These types of conversations ensure that your partner feels supported on an emotional level, as well as pleasured on a physical level.

Sometimes after sex, some people may experience feelings of rejection, isolation, loneliness, and even depression in some circumstances and that's rooted in the way their partner acts after sex. Following the act of sex, for some people, there is no emotional aftercare. Emotional aftercare in a sexual relationship means that you take the time to nurture each other after your orgasms, which allows you to leverage that oxytocin rush to feel a deep sense of connection with each other. When you skip this, the oxytocin floods, and you feel rejected because the bond is not being reciprocated. Spending time cuddling, helping each other get dressed, and expressing love and emotional intimacy is a beautiful way to take care of each other after sex. You can also spend time asking your partner questions and genuinely listening to them. Doing so helps you to better understand their sexual preferences and desires, which will bring you even closer together. When you share this communication and sexual aftercare with each other, sex goes from being a mere physical act of closeness to being an experience that deepens the bond between you and your partner.

Forgiveness Fans the Flame of Passion

Resentment and frustration can be deeply damaging to your sex life. When you feel angry toward your partner, mainly because you feel you have been wronged by them, it can feel uneasy about being naked with them. You might feel like being naked creates a high level of vulnerability that feels challenging or even unsafe to uphold. Learning how to forgive your partner quickly is a crucial step to preserve the sexual and emotional intimacy in the relationship.

Quick forgiveness does not mean you skip the steps of forgiveness, but that you do not prolong the process either. Rather than holding onto grudges or waiting an excessive period to discuss the troubles you have had, you make it a priority to talk about your hurt feelings and resolve them so you can move on from those troubles. This way, you are not making a habit of holding onto them and deepening the gap between yourself and your partner. Instead, you are releasing those feelings as soon as they arise and making a habit of maintaining a sense of closeness and loving connection between you and your partner. All this leads not only to the enrichment of your relationship but also to the improvement of your sex life.

Power of Non-sexual Touching

Physical intimacy is often viewed as being strictly sexual, but the reality is that physical intimacy can be far more than just intercourse. Everything from holding hands to offering massages, kissing, caressing, stroking each other's hair, and performing other physical acts of intimacy are all fantastic ways to grow your passion with your partner. These forms of intimacy may seem less important, but the reality is that they are equally as important as the sex itself.

When you have a healthy, thriving relationship, you can experience these sweet little acts of intimacy anywhere and anytime. If you are currently building your way back to a healthier relationship, these acts of intimacy can be used to create the foundation so that you feel increasingly more comfortable with your partner until the point where you are ready to have sex again.

I highly recommend you to work on educating yourself on all of the different types of non-sexual physical intimacy that you can engage in, as knowing all of the different ways can help you avoid falling into a routine and feeling bored in your non-sexual physical intimacy. This can happen, just like with sex, so changing it and doing it in different ways can spice it up. Some of the ways you can enjoy physical nonsexual intimacy include cuddling, kissing, brushing each other's hair, touching on the hand, shoulder, or arm when you are talking, holding hands, offering massages, hugging, or even just sitting shoulder to shoulder or playing footsies under the table. Another excellent way to share physical intimacy in your marriage is to take care of each other in a physical manner, such as showering together and washing each other off or applying lotion to each other's bodies. Although these acts may seem so simple, they can feel so passionate and intimate, plus that they can create a wonderful sense of support and connection in your marriage.

Separating Sex From Routines

Not having any sex at all can be devastating to a marriage, but so can sexual boredom. There are many reasons why partners may become stuck in boring sexual routines, ranging from comfort, familiarity, and habit, to trying to get pregnant or combatting fertility issues. Sexual routines often look like having sex at the same time, in the same way, or both. Regardless of how your sex has become monotonous, the experience itself can be extremely damaging to your sex life as it leads to dullness, less enjoyable orgasms, and a lack of excitement, interest and passion in your sex life.

Breaking the routine and having more enjoyable, spontaneous sex can help rekindle the passion in your marriage by offering you more powerful bonding experiences through sex. When sex is unpredictable, and you don't know what's coming up next, passion reignites, pleasure increases, orgasms become more intense, and you find yourself enjoying much greater intimacy and connection as a result of your sexual experiences.

Dropping the routine can be as simple as trying new positions, having sex in a new place or at an unusual time, or even engaging in fun stuff like role-playing or giving lingerie or sex toys a try in your sex life in order to spice things up a little bit. Remember that as long as you include spontaneity and unpredictability in sex, your sex life will always be spicy and passionate!

Emotional Intimacy and Sex

Love and sex do not have to coexist, but in a marriage, it's a must. Being able to experience emotional intimacy before, during, and after sex is a powerful way to strengthen your connection with your partner. Emotional intimacy can be incorporated into sex by discussing your feelings and emotions relating to sex itself and connecting over those feelings. You might let your partner know about how close and loved you feel, share about the joy or gratitude you feel through your bond, or otherwise talk about how good it feels to be so intimate with your partner. Speaking about these positive emotions is absolutely beneficial to your marriage and reminds your partner of the value and joy you both receive from being close in such a physical manner.

CHAPTER 10

Coping With Parenting Differences

If you have children, having different approaches in parenting can take a significant toll on your relationship. Having different opinions on how children should grow up makes raising your children more challenging than it really should be. You might find yourself growing angry or frustrated with your partner, arguing about parenting, competing with your partner or even undermining each other. These arguments can be highly stressful on your marriage and will definitely leave a negative traumatic impact on your children as they watch you argue always.

It's totally understandable that learning how to bridge the gap, cope with your differences, and parent as a team, when you have different opinions is challenging but certainly possible. There are plenty of practical steps you can take to help you heal this part of your marriage and make it have smooth sailing. It all starts with the willingness to come together, compromise, and make decisions that are beneficial for your children as well as for your marriage. Through healthy communication, consistency, and compromise, you can find an excellent balance in your parenting styles, and you can begin to enjoy a deeper sense of peace around this part of your marriage.

Discuss Your Parenting Expectations

Discussing your parenting expectations is so important an issue that should be done even long before you start trying to have children. Ideally, you should have already had these conversations; otherwise, you may realize later on that you are not on the same page, and that could absolutely create a considerable challenge for your family. Even if you did discuss these topics, however, you may find that your discussions were not entirely sufficient because things have changed since you had your children. This is absolutely normal and happens to the majority of parents as they realize that the reality of having children is much different than just the idea of having children.

It is a good idea to get into the habit of discussing your parenting expectations on a regular basis. This way, as they change, or as your child grows and new predicaments arise, you and your partner can share your opinions on what should be done to navigate those predicaments. Through these conversations, you will have a clearer idea of what your partner wants and needs, and they will have a clearer idea of what you want and need. You can also consider your children's wants or needs so you can find a happy medium for all of you, effectively leading you to the best solution for that stage of parenting.

Create Rules for Your Parenting Practices

Family rules and parenting rules are two excellent ways to start building a connection between your parenting style and your partner's parenting style. Family rules should define what everyone in the family is bound to uphold, while parenting rules should define what you and your partner are bound to uphold during parenting situations. Both of these serve an excellent purpose in your parenting experience, making it much easier for you to eliminate parenting-related fights from your marriage.

Family rules are excellent as they are rules that every member of the household needs to obey. These also help shape parenting rules, as they provide both parents with a clear understanding of what rules must be upheld, and they keep the rest of the household on track with those rules so that, hopefully, fewer disciplinary acts are required. Parenting rules, on the other hand, should be defined to help parents uphold the family rules, as well as navigate other aspects of your parenting journey together. For example, they should define what types of disciplinary acts are acceptable and which are not considered acceptable. They can also define what types of rewards are acceptable, how parenting decisions should be made, and other main aspects of parenting life. It goes without saying that the rules for your family will be different from the rules for other families; Therefore, consider your family's needs and create rules accordingly. All rules that go into your family and parenting rule guides should be approved by both parents to ensure both parents are satisfied with the parenting choices that are being made.

Determine Consequences Together

Delivering consequences as a parent unit is essential, especially when you are dealing with consequences on a more significant issue. Setting parenting rules can help manage smaller consequences that must be delivered at the moment, but for more prominent ones, deciding together is a meaningful way to navigate parenting. This ensures that both parents' concerns are met and that both parents agree with the consequences that have been delivered.

It is especially important to deliver consequences together if both parents have very different parenting approaches around the consequences themselves. For example, if one parent is more relaxed about consequences than the other, they must discuss this beforehand. This way, you can make compromises on the way discipline is delivered and provide it in a way that matches both parents' preferences and ultimately serves the child in learning the boundaries of their family and home.

Support Each Other in the Parenting Process

If you have children, you probably know that parenting is not easy, and there is no rule book that would work for everyone. There is no way to guarantee that what you are doing is right, nor is there any way to ensure that you will raise your kid precisely as you want to. You will feel angry, overwhelmed, disappointed, guilty, embarrassed, stressed, sad, and even miserable at times. Through all of it, though, you should trust that your partner is there and supporting you and willing to help you through the challenges. You should be able to talk to your partner about how challenging it is and to commit to making it easier for each other.

As you confide in each other about the parenting struggles you are facing, you should feel confident that your partner will look for opportunities to ease those challenges and cheer you on, helping to make parenting even more pleasant.

The reality is, you both contributed to the creation of your child. Or, if you are raising stepchildren, you both contribute to the creation of the home your children are being raised in. Both of you are equally important to those children's lives, and you both need to feel supported and capable of parenting in a healthy, fulfilling manner for everyone involved. By trusting that you have your partner's support, you build trust, emotional intimacy, and connection between you and your partner. Even if you have different approaches to parenting, never stop supporting each other along the way. Look for ways to ensure that needs of both you and your partner are met and that your children are growing happy and healthy. The more you can create this type of environment, the more enriching your home life will be, the better your parenting will be, and the stronger your marriage will be.

Never Disagree in Front of Your Children

While you never want to hide reality from your children, it is always a good idea to avoid having severe disagreements or discussions in front of your children, particularly around the subject of parenting. Showing children how to disagree on topics like what to have for dinner or where to take your next vacation is vital as it teaches them how to navigate disagreements in a healthy way. However, disagreeing about parenting specifically in front of your children will result in your children taking note of the discrepancies and using it to their advantage. Unfortunately, because they do not realize it is not correct to behave this way, many children will manipulate their parents this way in order to get what they want.

Unless something genuinely abusive or wrong is going on, take note of the disagreement and wait until a later time to bring it up with your partner in private. Discuss it with them when the children cannot hear, and have an honest and respectful discussion about why you disagree and how you would have preferred things to be done. You can then discuss the ideal way for such things to be handled in the future so that both partners know how to handle those problems next time. This ensures that you are on the same page and supporting each other without creating space for disharmony or lies in your family unit.

Be Flexible With Your Parenting Style

As a parent, you should continually reassess your parenting style to ensure that it continues to match your children's needs and interests. The ideas and beliefs you had before having children most probably have changed once they came into your life. The reality of having children, combined with the different personalities and needs of each child, can vastly change one's opinion on parenting and how it should proceed.

Being flexible as a parent is essential for your children, but it is also crucial for your marriage. You need to be flexible enough to adapt your parenting style to match your children's needs while also being able to compromise with your partner's needs and desires. As your child grows, work with your partner to find common ground in your parenting style that will fit your children and help them grow in the best manner possible. This way, you are contributing to parenting in the healthiest manner possible.

Always Give Second Chances

Both you and your partner will make many mistakes in parenting. You may make a wrong decision or lose your cool, or you may do something that totally misses the mark and leads to a crummy situation for everyone. When your partner makes a mistake, avoid jumping straight into accusations and anger and putting your partner down for the mistake they have made. First, they have already become aware of their mistakes, and they are looking for ways to improve their parenting style and to avoid making such mistakes again. Second, they need you to support them, not hold them back from being able to grow as a parent.

Remember that your partner is your partner, not your enemy. Although you want to protect your children with everything you have, you need to remember that they do too, and you need to be ready to sit back and trust your partner and hold space for them to navigate the world of parenting. Look for ways to get on your partner's side and help them when they have made a mistake, and always do everything in your power to make it better with them. When you and your partner both realize you have someone right there helping you through those challenges,

ALICE GARDNER

it becomes much easier to navigate them and grow as a couple and as a family.

Chapter 11

Following Healthy Habits

After you have successfully taken the seven steps to fix your marriage, there are additional steps you can take to keep your marriage at its best. At this point, you want to focus on developing healthy, long-lasting habits that will ensure that you continue to grow and flourish as a couple. Remember that fixing a marriage is not just about fixing your problems; it's about creating a stronger foundation so that whenever a challenging situation comes along, you know how to manage it and move on. The more you can focus on continuing to grow and nourish your relationship, the longer your relationship will last.

Understand that in every relationship, even the healthiest ones, disagreements occur, and everyone will find themselves frustrated and dealing with challenges from time to time. However, healthy relationships will have certain habits that enable them to navigate these challenging times in a peaceful, healthy and effective manner so they can refrain from allowing them to hold them back ultimately. Further, you can use these skills to help make your great times even better and also grow as a couple.

What I teach you in this chapter is the sum of the essential skills from the previous chapters. What you are supposed to do is to turn them into effective day-to-day practices and utilize them to help you strengthen your marriage. I recommend you routinely check-in to ensure you are still following them and that they are working since this is fundamental if you want to have a healthy marriage in the future.

Talk on a Daily Basis

As I said previously, communication is one of the most critical elements of any marriage. You must talk in order to get through your struggles and fix the relationship that has been broken; otherwise, you will never get there. Without communication, you will never know where your partner is at, what they are thinking, or what they need. Aside from using communication to manage your problems, you need to use communication in order to come closer together as a couple as well.

I suggest you talk about your day, the goings-on at work, and any funny stories you may have from your day or your week. Share the small, seemingly meaningless aspects of your days, as this is a wonderful way to let your partner know that you were thinking about them and wanted to bring them into your day to day experience, even if they couldn't physically be there. When you talk about these things, you and your partner gain the opportunity to get to know each other more on a day to day basis, which allows you to grow closer and stay familiar with each other's lives. This way, rather than growing apart, you grow closer together.

Schedule Time for Each Other

Intimacy has to be the number one priority in your marriage; that's why you need to dedicate your time and energy to deepen emotional as well as physical intimacy every single day if you want to maintain a strong connection with your partner. These types of intimacy do not require deep conversations until three o'clock in the morning or having sex every day to be maintained. Every day, look for a way to develop your intimacy with each other in unique, fulfilling manners. Spend time thinking about it, planning for it, and putting your energy into creating these moments. The energy you invest in your marriage will always be repaid tenfold in the level of connection and joy you gain from your marriage.

For emotional intimacy, make an effort to talk to your partner, let them know you cherish them and are grateful for them, and ask them about themselves. Spend time listening to their day, understanding what was important to them, and showing interest in the things they do. If they tell you about a story that builds on something they were previously talking about, such as something going on at work, show that you care by remembering what they told you and engaging back in the conversation. Creating this emotional intimacy is extremely useful for your connection with each other.

For physical intimacy, make time to take care of each other, rub each other's backs or feet, or lotion each other. Take a shower together, hold hands, hug, or even just cuddle on the couch while you are watching TV after a long day. If you feel touched out because you are exhausted from the children, hold hands on the couch, or touch each other's feet and create that sense of closeness. Fall asleep holding each other, or at least facing each other. These little gestures of intimacy will nurture your marriage in a powerful, long-lasting way.

Kiss Each Other Every Day

When you first start dating someone, all you might think of is planting a kiss on them. You want to kiss them when you greet each other or when you are saying goodbye, and at any chance, you get in between. Over time, kisses may feel like they lose that novelty, and they may slowly start to fall to the wayside. You might stop kissing each other when you get home from work or before you leave, or making time for kisses when you are just lounging around together. It is essential, though, that you don't let kissing end.

Studies have shown that similar to orgasms, kissing can release oxytocin and create a deeper bond between two partners. When you kiss and feel that physical touch, you deepen your connection while also letting your partner know that you still love them and are crazy for them. Make time for kissing every single day and, while you are at it, don't be afraid to get into a hot and heavy make-out session every now and then. These steamy kisses can quickly rekindle the passion in your marriage and even leave you both craving for more.

Consult One Another

When you are in a marriage, you are in a partnership with another individual, and you have both committed to growing together. Regardless of how you do it, there will be extremely close-knit aspects of your lives in virtually every area of your life. Even areas of your life that do not directly involve your partner, such as your career, are affected by your partner and will have an impact on your marriage; consequently, so you need to be aware of this, and you should be considerate to your partner when making choices.

Consulting your partner does not necessarily mean asking for their permission, as you never need their 'OK' to make a choice for yourself. However, it does mean that you value your partner enough to consider their opinions, concerns, and needs, and you make decisions that ultimately benefit both of you in a positive manner. Anytime you have a choice to make about family, religion, career, travel, or anything else that will directly affect your partner, always consult your partner first. Going to your partner for advice shows that you care about them and their opinions and that you do respect them. This also shows that you will always make an active effort to ensure that they have a say in family matters and that they contribute to the lifestyle you are building together.

Openly Express Your Gratitude

After many years together, it is natural for couples to develop insecurities about being appreciated. This feeling can lead to partners seeking positive affection from outside their marriage since they worry that their partner no longer values them and loves them the way they once did. Expressing gratitude for your partner is a healthy way to remind them that they still mean the world to you and that you cherish everything they do for you and your family. Never be afraid to express your gratitude. Thank your partner for all the things they have done for you and your family, all the love they have given to you so far, and all the way they have come with you through thick and thin.

When you express your gratitude to your partner, do not focus solely on what they do for you or your family. Focus on the things they do for themselves and the ways they make themselves better as well. Express gratitude for their healthy lifestyle choices, their excellent qualities, and who they are as a person. The more you can show appreciation for your partner and deeply value them, the more they will feel supported by you. This way, they turn to you for positive attention, affection and appreciation, because they know that you are the one who has plenty for them.

Genuinely Listen to Your Partner

Talking to your partner and opening up about your life is not the only way you can take care of your marriage on a daily basis. Another important way to take care of your marriage is to genuinely listen to your partner and to listen well. When your partner pours their heart out to you, listen. When they share stories from their day or say something that they think would make you laugh, pay attention.

As you listen, put your phone down, put distractions away, and listen with your full being. Face your partner, look into their eyes, and hear all of the words they are saying. Pay attention to how they express themselves with their words, voice, and body language, and allow yourself to fully grasp everything that is being said to you. This way, you have a deeper sense of understanding and a more remarkable ability to connect to your partner through the words they are sharing. Always reassure your partner that you are listening by affirming what you have heard and responding in a way that clearly answers any questions they may have had and provide feedback on what they were talking about. According to research, listening well and giving feedback is proved to be a great way of strengthening the connection and emotional bond between two partners. So go for it!

Go on Regular Dates

Do you remember when you and your partner first met, and you went on dates to get to know each other and to spend as much time with each other as possible? Before you lived together, dates and sleepovers were outstanding as they were the time you had specifically set aside to spend together, and you spent a significant amount of time anticipating and preparing for those dates. When you had them, they felt so special, and you were excited every time you could share this experience with your partner. You couldn't wait to see them again. Good old days, Right? Don't worry; you can make those days happen again.

I know, now that you are married, it may seem more challenging to create this excitement around your dates, but it doesn't have to be. Just because you see your partner every day and you spend most of your time together does not mean that you cannot have specific dates and get excited again about having quality time together. Even if you do not have children, go on dates that take you away from your everyday life and create a meaningful time for each other. This time will carry the same special feeling with it and will encourage you to remember why you fell in love in the first place, effectively keeping your intimate connection strong.

Spend Time Reminiscing

Reminiscing is surprisingly powerful for your marriage. Whether you have been together for only a few months or several years, there are plenty of positive, fun-filled memories you can reminisce on together. Reminiscing is a great habit because it allows you to relive happy memories and, as a result, reabsorb the incredible energy and emotions that came with making those happy memories. Be sure to let your partner in on your thoughts and feelings from those days, and let them know about the way they made you feel. They may not have known what exactly you were thinking or feeling, and hearing about your shared memories through your perspective is a wonderful way to bring them into your experience while also replaying happy times in your life.

While you do not have to reminisce every single day, it feels good to spend some time reliving your memories through your spouse's eyes. Hearing about what was special for them and how excited they were, or how much they cherished certain aspects of your shared experience increases how wonderful those memories are for you, and will do the same for them when you share your experiences as well. If you are going through hard times together, make a point to reminisce on your happier memories so you can enjoy those positive feelings together. It will go a long way toward helping you move beyond those struggles and rebuild your marriage.

Chapter 12

Keeping Your Marriage Off Life Support

Maintaining your marriage is essential, but once you have reached the point where you have had severe troubles, it is essential that you learn how to keep your marriage off life support, which will be possible through adjusting your perspective and maintaining mindfulness around your marriage so you can keep it from going astray. When you are able to be aware and mindful of the troubles you have previously faced, it tremendously helps with preventing further marital problems.

Keeping your marriage off life support by taking these preventative measures will also prove to your partner that you want to enjoy a strong, healthy relationship with them; that is when your partner sees you putting in a genuine effort to keep everything positive and loving, they will appreciate your efforts and feel even more devoted to nurturing your marriage. The end result is a marriage that never again finds itself on the verge of falling apart.

Commit Seriously to Your Marriage

First and foremost, you need to commit seriously to your marriage. You married your partner because you love them, so you need to take that commitment seriously and put continuous energy into maintaining your marriage. If you allow ideas to flood your mind about you being happier without your marriage, even if you never openly voice those thoughts, it can cause a serious strain on your marriage. The thought alone can prevent you from putting all of your energy into fixing your marriage and can result in your marriage starting to break down.

Anytime you find yourself feeling as though you would be better off without your partner, talk to your partner about that. Reaffirm your commitment by taking this as a sign that you need to improve your marriage and not as evidence that it is time for your marriage to end. Let your partner know what you need, and look for ways to fulfill those needs together, rather than allowing yourself to feed into the belief that you would be happier without them. By doing this, you decide ahead of time that divorce is not an option, and you look for solutions, rather than allowing yourself to start toying with the idea of separation.

Respect and Honor Your Partner

Marriage is supposed to last decades, and over the course of those years, it is inevitable that you, your partner or both of you will grow and change. If your marriage withstands the test of time, you need to learn to respect and honor each other through understanding and adapting to all of the changes you come across through the years. What I'm saying is not suggesting you only tolerate those changes, but learn to truly appreciate them and love every version of your partner that you come to know through the course of your lifetime together. The more you fall in love with each version of your partner, the more you will remember why you fell in love in the first place and that love can withstand everything.

Anytime you witness a change in your partner that you do not particularly like, do not become fearful or defensive or try to prevent them from making those changes. Instead, learn to accept these aspects and trust that this is all a part of who they are, and that you can love them without having to love every single aspect of them. Show support in every way you can, and always vocalize your needs and concerns in a respectful and compassionate way if any of their changes negatively affect you or your marriage. This way, you are respecting and honoring your partner while also respecting and honoring yourself.

Schedule Time for Honest Communication

Daily communication helps, but so do regular check-ins to see how things are going. Sometimes, day to day conversations may not feel like the right time to bring up big problems, even if you intend to talk about them at some point with your partner. You might find yourself not wanting to talk about them because you worry that doing so will disrupt an otherwise wonderful day or will make a bad day worse. Rather than trying to decide when to talk, have times scheduled for when you will discuss your marriage and how things are going. Use this as an opportunity to let your partner know what you are concerned with, what needs are not being met, or what can be done to improve the quality of your relationship. This way, you had already intended to talk to your partner at this time, and you are not springing it into an average day and dealing with the possibly unwanted repercussions of that choice.

Share Your Financial Expectations

Finances can break a marriage. In fact, they are one of the leading causes of divorce, often because one or both partners have vastly different opinions on finances than their partner does. For example, one partner may be a lavish spender while the other is frugal and likes to save, or one may be trying to make ends meet while the other seems oblivious to what is going on in their finances and spends everything they have. It is not uncommon for one partner to be more frivolous with money and the other to be more fearful or stressed around money. It is also not uncommon for both partners to be fearful and stressed around money and to feel aggravated by their partner, who may share different beliefs around what is worth the investment and what is not.

Money talks should be done before you ever get married, but they should also be shared consistently throughout your marriage. Regularly discuss your budget, anything affecting your finances, and the financial goals you have created together. The more you communicate about finances, compromise and create a plan that works for both of you, and stay on the same page about this issue, the stronger your marriage will be.

Make Space for Yourselves and Each Other

Intentionally devoting your time toward your independence and your marriage is an excellent way to avoid running into trouble in your marriage. Even if you do not feel like you need more time apart or together, it is crucial to be mindful of how that time accumulates. It may not seem like a big deal to only spend time together in the evenings or to give up on dating and relish in day to day experiences together, but the reality is that dating matters. Dating tells your partner that you still value special time together and that they are still worth the effort you spend on planning an unforgettable time together. Likewise, planning a particular time for yourself lets you know that you can still trust and rely on yourself and that you do not need your partner to be present in order for you to be happy and have a good time.

Each week, look at the calendar and look for opportunities to spend time with your partner and on your own. Ideally, each day should include some time for your partner and some time for yourself, and each week should include one or two events that involve more significant time with your partner and with yourself. This keeps a healthy balance between how you invest your time and allows you to prevent yourself from feeling overwhelmed by your marriage or by your amount of time spent alone. Instead of finding yourself on life support because you feel suffocated or underappreciated, you find yourself feeling cherished and having plenty of space to be by yourself as well.

Manage Your Wellness Together

Managing your wellness together has a surprisingly powerful impact on your marriage, as it allows you and your partner to remain transparent and honest with where you stand in your marriage. It also gives you a unique look into where your partner's strengths and weaknesses are and allows you to get on board with helping them fortify their strengths and offset their weaknesses. In addition, when you exercise, you feel more attractive and energized, which makes it easier for you to feel a sense of security and courage around your partner. Even years into a relationship, you may still find that you feel insecure about your partner at times and that your partner feels insecure with you. When you take the time to learn how to manage your wellness together, motivate each other, and meet your goals together, you offset those insecurities by putting in regular effort toward feeling better within yourself and helping your partner feel better too.

Moreover, spending time together by working out is a wonderful way to share something special with your partner. So, try to have some 'together time' in your weekly schedule, even if you find your life cramped and busy; this allows you to focus on both your health and your marriage. You can join a class together, go to the gym together, or take up the same sport or fitness practice. You can either set independent goals such as to gain more muscle or lose weight or set a mutual goal such as running a marathon together. Either way, you can motivate each other toward your goals and celebrate each other for all the milestones you achieve.

Work on Forgiving Each Other Quickly

Needless to say that hardships exist in every marriage and every life, but if you let your marriage continue to suffer in the face of a challenge, only because you find it too difficult to move on, or you simply do not want to, you are choosing to let your marriage remain complicated. You need to decide to forgive each other and learn to move on from troubles quickly. At first, this may take time, as you need to rebuild trust, and of course, quickly moving on requires trust in your partner. You need to trust that your partner did not intend to hurt you and that they will do better in the future because they want to respect you and improve your relationship together. Once you have reached that level of trust, forgiving becomes a habit!

As soon as you overcome a problem with your partner, focus on remembering why you love your partner and get in the mindset of believing the best in your partner. Trust that they meant no harm and that they will do better, and have the necessary conversation to get you to that point. Then, go ahead and commit to forgiving your partner and moving on from that conversation so you can begin loving each other once again. The sooner you have these talks, commit to forgiveness, and move on, the stronger your marriage will be in the long run.

Avoid Trying to Control Each Other

Marriages can be full of power struggles and controlling behaviors if both partners are not careful. This stems from the fact that marriages are full of vulnerability, and when the vulnerability is a concern, people naturally become more controlling as they attempt to prevent themselves from being hurt. You may try to control your partner, and vice versa, in an effort to prevent them from taking actions that lead to hurt feelings.

Remember that at the end of the day, everyone should be the way they want to be, and nobody is obligated to be controlling about the other's behaviors and identity in general. You must be your authentic selves, and you consciously choose to love each other and build your lives together as two authentic individuals that are in love.

When it comes to controlling, ensure that you do not try to monitor to control each other's actions or decisions. Understand that while you can have an opinion, it is not up to you to know what is going on at all times, nor do you get the final say in your partner's decisions. Give your partner space to be their authentic self, and learn to collaborate on decisions by being two independent persons, rather than by trying to get your partner to do everything your way. Also, give your spouse the freedom to do what they want without having to ask for permission. Of course, they may tell you what is going on for courtesy purposes, but they SHOULD NOT have to ask if it is okay to go somewhere or do something without you. If you let control to take any space in your marriage, you will be far more likely to find yourself in an emotionally, mentally, financially, or even physically abusive marriage, which will almost certainly lead to divorce.

Keep Practicing Healthier Marital Skills

Just because you have found your way through your initial troubles does not mean you are in the clear yet. In fact, your work is never truly done. You need to continue practicing healthier marital skills on a daily basis. Anytime you have your regular check-ins to discuss your marriage, look for healthy coping methods for any problems you may be facing. If you notice that something in your marriage is not necessarily a problem but that it could be more severe, put effort into doing better in that area before it becomes a real thing.

Routinely working on doing better in your marriage will always allow you to experience improvements while also allowing you to quickly recognize any area that needs work. This way, you can keep your marriage off life support and continually make it the strongest marriage possible. In the end, you both win, and the prize will be enjoying the most fulfilling and enriching marriage that you could have ever dreamed of.

Conclusion

Congratulations on completing *Fix Your Marriage in 7 Steps!*

This book was written to help you save your marriage from whatever troubles you might be facing right now, no matter how big or small they may be.

I hope that through reading this book you have discovered the importance of taking action to repair, maintain, and grow your relationship over time. Throughout this guide, the first steps have been clearly defined for you, and now, it is time for you to take the necessary actions if you're really willing to experience the marriage of your dreams. You need to discover how you can maintain the day to day balance of your marriage, while also being mindful so as to avoid running into new problems with your partner. The more you create these habits of fixing, maintaining, and preventing troubles, the stronger your marriage will be as you will regularly be putting work into making it better.

After reading this book, you may be feeling many different things. You might be feeling excited, accomplished, and as though you have a renewed sense of hope in your marriage. You might also be feeling overwhelmed, frustrated, or like your marriage is so far from excellent that you question whether it is worth salvaging or not. I want you to remember that it is totally normal to feel a sense of hope as well as doubt, especially when your marriage has gone through so much damage and now, obviously, you are feeling sort of insecure from the troubles you have encountered. However, you only need to know that experiencing these feelings is OK and want to decide to resolve the conflicts.

The next step is to take these actions seriously and commit to engaging in them every single day. Look for ways to show appreciation and gratitude to your partner, rebuild your trust, emotional intimacy, and physical passion. You also need to regularly nurture the life you have together. As you continue to rebuild your relationship, try to find new methods to grow even closer, and make improving your marriage your lifelong mission. The more energy you put into your marriage, the more fulfillment and satisfaction you will get out of it.

Aside from working on your marriage, I also encourage you to take time to work on yourself as well. Having challenges in your marriage can lead to a variety of painful feelings, and at times, it may even drive you away from your real sense of self. Taking the time to genuinely focus on yourself and your well-being enables you to heal from the harm you have experienced in your marriage. As you discover how to feel healed within yourself, approaching your marriage through a healed heart and a peaceful mind becomes more effortless. Remember, in any relationship, you are one of the two parties, and you need to feel capable of showing up in that relationship if you want to enjoy a healthier connection with the other person. Be honest and approachable in your healing journey, and this will significantly aid your well-being, as well as the health of your marriage.

Before closing the book, I want you to take one last action. That is, stop and look at your partner and let them know how much you love and cherish them. Thank them for being there with you and being willing to figure this out with you. The fact that you have both committed to this process and that you have made it this far proves your devotion to each other, and that is worth expressing gratitude for. Spend some time showing your love and appreciation to your partner and also engaging in the skills you have discovered in this very book. I consider doing this as the real first step to heal and move on!

As well, if you could take a moment to review *Fix Your marriage in 7 Steps* on Amazon Kindle, your honest feedback would be much appreciated.

Thank you, and best of luck! I bet you can do it!

First of all, thank you for purchasing Fix Your Marriage in 7 Steps. I know you could have picked any number of books to read, but you picked this book, and for that I am incredibly grateful. I hope that it added value and quality to your everyday life. If so, it would be really nice if you could share this book with your friends and family by posting on , Instagram and .

If you enjoyed this book and found some benefit in reading this, I'd like to hear from you and hope that you could take some time to post a review on Amazon. Your feedback and support will help me to improve his writing craft significantly for future projects and make this book even better. I wish you the best in all that you do!

Customer Reviews

☆☆☆☆☆ 38
4.8 out of 5 stars ▼

5 star	▬▬▬▬	87%
4 star	▪	10%
3 star	▫	3%
2 star		0%
1 star		0%

Share your thoughts with other customers

Write a customer review

See all 38 customer reviews ›

About the Author

Alice Gardner is a psychologist with over 20 years of experience in couples counseling and individual psychotherapy.

Born in Colorado, she moved to Chicago to complete her studies in psychology; Alice's interest in the relationships between couples began when she worked as a volunteer counselor while still at university.

In her practice, she uses a range of proven approaches to help couples heal and reconnect, having committed herself to a life of learning. Known for her empathy and appealing personality, Alice's ability to help people to address the critical issues that couples confront nowadays has had an intense and transformative effect on many of her clients' lives.

Alice Gardner has helped countless couples gain insight into their problems, resolve ongoing conflict, rebuild sexual connection, and develop long-lasting relationships. In her books, she explores the roots of couples' issues and offers sensible and essential advice about how to deal with them.

She is the author of numerous self-help books that help people overcome obstacles that stand in the way.

Alice lives in Northern California with her husband, their two children, and a Labrador.

www.bonusliber.com

Other Alice Gardner's Books

***

Reconnect With Your Partner

A Couples Communication Workbook to Build Intimacy, Resolve Conflicts and Make Your Relationship Stronger

***

Healing From Infidelity

How to Recover from the Heartbreak Caused by Your Partner's Affair, Rebuild Trust and Save Your Relationship

***

Recupérate de la Infidelidad (Spanish Edition)

Cómo Reponerse de la Desilusión Causada por la Infidelidad de tu Pareja, Recuperar la Confianza y Salvar tu Relación

***

Marriage Counseling Made Easy

The 3-in-1 Guide to Couples Therapy. How to Recover After Infidelity, Improve Couples Communication Skills and Build a Healthy Relationship with Your Spouse

Made in the USA
Las Vegas, NV
03 April 2023